Bittker and Eustice

FEDERAL INCOME TAXATION OF CORPORATIONS AND SHAREHOLDERS

SEVENTH EDITION

JAMES S. EUSTICE
Gerald L. Wallace Professor of Taxation
New York University

REVISED STUDY PROBLEMS

WARREN, GORHAM & LAMONT
OF RIA

Preface

CORPORATE TAXATION is a difficult but exciting subject. It requires the student to apply all of the tools of the lawyer's art to some of the most difficult brain teasers to be found in the law. And yet there is a satisfying coherence and unity in the law of corporate taxation, which when grasped by the student can make the exercise well worth the effort.

I have drawn these assignments and problems from my experience, assignments, and problems used in forty-plus years of teaching corporate taxation at New York University School of Law. These problems do not teach the course but should aid instructors in fashioning a course composed of selected lessons and parts of lessons. The material here is far more extensive than will be assigned in most courses, and the student should not feel obligated to push beyond the assigned portion. The lessons labeled "Advanced" are not the only ones that may be deleted from the usual J.D.-level course.

Students presumably will have had at least an introductory course in federal income taxation before taking a course based on these lessons. Nevertheless, students will likely feel that the subject matter here is different in kind and intensity, and they will most likely be correct. Therefore, I encourage students to hit the ground running in their corporate tax course and not slip behind. It is very difficult to wrap one's mind around material of this complexity for the first time toward the end of the semester in review.

I wish to thank Jasper Cummings for his invaluable assistance on the earlier version of these problems.

JAMES S. EUSTICE

Table of Contents

STUDY PROBLEMS

Introduction

As a convention in the problems, X, Y, Z, P (parent), S (subsidiary), and T (target) refer to corporate taxpayers. Individual taxpayers are A, B, C, or D. A lender or creditor is L; in Lesson 16, L is a corporation with losses. A partnership is A-B. When visualizing these entities, it is helpful to make corporations squares, individuals circles, and partnerships, trusts, and estates diamonds. A relatively new player in the world of subchapter C, the disregarded entity (or "DE"), can be represented by a cloud. Assume corporate taxpayers are taxed at a flat 35 percent rate on all income, unless otherwise indicated. While state income taxes can be very important, they are ignored for purposes of this course. Similarly, foreign tax issues are very important, but I will assume that all persons and activities are domestic, that is, in the United States. When problem answers involve income, it generally will be sufficient to state the amount and type without calculating the tax, unless otherwise indicated. In the few cases where an individual's tax must be computed, assume a 35 percent rate on all income, except where the capital gains rate is clearly applicable (15 percent). Since 2003, however, dividends also qualify for the lower capital gain rates. Assume that all assets are capital assets in the hands of their owners, unless the facts or context clearly indicate otherwise. Also assume that there are no tax-relevant transactions for the year other than those stated. In addition, assume that all taxpayers report on the calendar year, all corporations use the accrual method of accounting, and all individuals use the cash method of accounting. Assume that all of the stock of a corporation is worth the same as the value of all of its assets net of liabilities. References to "income" may refer to gross or net income, as appropriate, but when referring to net income also include a possible net loss.

The enumerated questions that follow a set of assumptions are alternatives and are not cumulative, unless otherwise noted.

Be aware that some of the assigned Treasury regulations may be out of date, and so may not agree with the related Internal Revenue Code sections; the Code controls. Always check for the existence of proposed and temporary regulations that may affect the assigned regulations. Assume that each assignment includes the current "no-ruling revenue procedure," which is generally numbered "3" for the year (e.g., Rev. Proc. 2002-3).

STUDY PROBLEMS

Note: Legislation enacted in 2003 reducing the top rate on dividends to 15 percent (the same rate as capital gains, likewise reduced to 15 percent) will have a major impact on Lessons 5, 6, 7A, and 7B (as well as other provisions dealt with in this course).

Your instructor will select the particular lessons to be studied and their order. In so doing, the instructor may also downsize the lesson by directing you to disregard certain problems and parts of the assigned Code sections, and so forth.

COMMONLY USED ACRONYMS AND TERMS

AAA   accumulated adjustments account (§ 1368(c)(1))

A/B   adjusted basis (§§ 1012, 1016)

AFR   applicable federal rate (§ 1274(d))

AMT   alternative minimum tax (§ 55)

B&E   Student Edition of Federal Income Taxation of Corporations and Shareholders (Seventh Edition) by Boris I. Bittker and James S. Eustice [assignments to B&E always include the related portions of its current supplement]

COD   cancellation of indebtedness (or discharge of indebtedness) income (§ 61(a)(12))

DE   a disregarded entity for federal income tax purposes

Disposition No. 1

the transfer of assets by a corporation in a reorganization

Disposition No. 2

the transfer of stock, securities, and possibly other property by a corporation as a second step in a reorganization following Disposition No. 1

Disposition No. 3

the transfer of stock or securities by a holder in exchange for the transfer made by a corporation in its Disposition No. 2

DRD   dividends-received deduction (§ 243)

E&P   earnings and profits (usually used in the singular) (§ 312)

FMV   fair market value

GU   General Utilities & Operating Co. v. Helvering, 296 US 200 (1935)

IP   issue price (§§ 1273, 1274)

LBO   leveraged buyout

NEED   not essentially equivalent to a dividend (§ 302(b)(1))

NOL   net operating loss (§ 172)

NQP   nonqualified preferred stock

OID   original issue discount (§§ 1272–1275); OID equals SRPM less IP

SRPM   stated redemption price at maturity (§ 1273(a)(2))

STD   step transaction doctrine

TVM   time value of money, reflected in OID

Introductory/
Definition of "Corporation"

SUBJECT: Identifying the corporation as a taxable entity for federal tax purposes—Determining when the corporation will be treated as the earner of income—Overview of the income taxing regimes—The current world of "status electivity" for noncorporate business entities (check-the-box regime)

ASSIGNMENT

B&E: ¶¶ 1.01, 1.05, 2.01, 2.02, 2.03, 2.04, 2.05, 2.06, 2.07, 2.10

Code: §§ 11(a), 7701(a)(1), 7701(a)(2), 7701(a)(3), 7701(a)(14), 7704(a), 7704(b)

Regs: §§ 301.7701-1, 301.7701-2(a)–301.7701-2(c), 301.7701-3(a)–301.7701-3(b)(1), 301.7701-4(a)–301.7701-4(c)(1)

PROBLEMS

(1)   Two individuals, *A* and *B*, want to form a new business venture, invest $5,000 each in it, and raise additional capital of $10 million from either a handful or thousands of investors. What are the three principal alternative regimes in the Code for taxing the business income that might be earned by such venture (identify by subchapter name)? Which of these regimes requires the business entity to pay tax on the income earned by the business? Which of these regimes requires the entity's owners to pay tax on the income earned by the entity?

(2)   *A* and *B* may organize one of the following entities to operate their business venture. Which of the the following entities will the Code necessarily treat as

a corporation? Which can the Code treat as a corporation, if the entity so elects? Assume for these questions that the investors number either 10 or 10,000 (in which case the equity units are publicly traded).

(a)   A corporation chartered under the Delaware corporate laws.

(b)   A general partnership.

(c)   A limited partnership.

(d)   A limited liability company organized under the Delaware LLC statute.

(e)   A trust of which *A* and *B* are the trustees and the investors are "beneficiaries."

(3)   *X* owns 100 percent of an LLC. How will the income of the LLC be taxed if the LLC makes no election?

ADD TO ASSIGNMENT

Cases: CIR v. Bollinger, 485 US 340 (1988); Charles Johnson, 78 TC 882 (1982)

(4)   *A* and *B* organize a Delaware corporation for the business (having obtained no investors) but continue to operate the business under its pre-incorporation name, "A&B Enterprises," continue to use the pre-incorporation bank account, make contracts for the incorporated business in their own names as individuals, and generally ignore the incorporation except for depositing receipts in a corporate bank account and paying themselves "salary" (but with no employment contract or board resolution) and filing a corporate income tax return as a C corporation. Could the Service assess *A* and *B* for tax on the "corporate income"? Should it do so?

(5)   *A* and *B* are surgeons who form a professional corporation under the laws of their state, which laws require that licensed professionals own all of the stock

of the corporation. The corporation's income consists entirely of charges for operations *A* and *B* perform. All activities are carried out in the name of the corporation. Who owns the income from operations; what other facts may be relevant to answer this question?

(6)   *A-B* partnership was formed to own and operate an apartment project. Because of local usury laws, it was necessary that corporation *X* (owned by unrelated persons) be utilized to hold legal title to the property as a "nominee" (or straw person) for the benefit of *A-B*. Does *A-B* want *X* to be treated as the owner of the project for federal income tax purposes, and, if not, will *A-B* get the result it wants?

Alternative: The partners of *A-B* own all the stock of *X*.

The Corporation Income Tax

2A   Overview; Stakes and Comparison of S Corporation Regime

SUBJECT: Comparison of various taxing regimes in the Code—Application of the corporate tax rate—Consideration of the advisability of an S election

ASSIGNMENT

B&E: ¶¶ 1.02, 1.03, 1.04, 1.07, 5.01–5.03[1], 5.09, 6.01, 6.02, 6.06, 6.08, 6.11, 7.01

Code: §§ 1(a)–1(e), 1(h), 11, 162(a)(1), 701, 702, 1014, 1201(a), 1211(a), 1361(a), 1361(b)(1), 1361(b)(2), 1363(a), 1363(b), 1366(a), 1366(b), 1366(d)(1), 1367(a), 1371(a)

PROBLEMS

(1)   *Focus on the short term:* If *A*, an entertainer, were averaging $1 million a year of taxable income from his business, would you advise *A* to incorporate as a device to save taxes? Would you advise *A* to make an S election for the corporation? To help you answer these questions, compare the net after-tax cash *A* would have after a full year (a) as a sole proprietor, (b) as the shareholder and only employee of an S corporation that pays him a $1 million salary, or (c) as the shareholder and only employee of a C corporation that pays him all of its after-tax income as salary. Would he do better if he used a C corporation that paid him a $500,000 salary and he either received the maximum possible dividend or sold the stock the next year? What would result if he took a $500,000 salary from his S corporation and sold the stock the next year?

(2)   *Focus on the longer term: A* wants to organize a manufacturing business that will generate $1 million in taxable income per year without any reinvestment of income. After-tax income can also earn 10 percent in the second and third years by being reinvested in the business (in capital equipment, so there will be no accumulated earnings tax for a C corporation problem if dividends are

not paid). Calculate the aggregate after-tax income of the business at the end of the third year, assuming first that the business operates as an S corporation or a limited liability company (here, the calculation will be at A's level) and second that the business operates as a C corporation (here, the calculation will be at the corporation's level; assume no dividends). Does your calculation mean that the business should operate as a C corporation? Would your answer change if you assume that A sells the business at the end of the third year or dies at the end of Year 3 and leaves the ownership of the business to either A's spouse or A's son?

2B   Dividends-Received Deduction; § 1059

SUBJECT: Introduction to multiple corporation tax issues—How the computation of corporate taxable income is affected by intercorporate dividends, which provides a convenient opportunity to introduce the interplay of § 243 with § 1059

ASSIGNMENT

B&E: ¶¶ 5.01, 5.05, 13.02, 13.40, 13.43[3][a]

Code: §§ 11(a), 11(b), 61(a)(3), 61(a)(7), 63(a), 241, 243(a)–243(c), 246(b), 246(c), 246A(a)–246A(b), 1001, 1012, 1059(a)–1059(e)(2), 1211(a), 1222(2), 1501, 1504(a)(1), 1504(a)(2), 1561(a), 1563(a)

PROBLEMS

(1) X is a publicly held corporation with a subsidiary, S, of which X always has owned 100 percent of the outstanding stock. What is the total tax liability for X and S under each of the following sets of facts? (In this problem, use all corporate tax rate brackets.)

(a) X has taxable income of $2.2 million and S has no income.

(b) X has taxable income of $2 million and S has taxable income of $200,000.

(c)   Same as (b) above, but S distributed $100,000 to X as a dividend.

(d)   Same as (c) above, but X has not always owned all of the stock of S, and the dividend is distributed out of earnings and profits of a taxable year of S during which S and X were not members of the same affiliated group.

(e)   Same as (c) above, but *X* owns only 10 percent of the vote and value of *S*'s stock at all times during the year.

(f)   Same as (c) above, but *X* and *S* file a consolidated return.

(2)   *Y* learns that *X* (a large public company) will pay a large dividend, and so, before the record date, *Y* buys one share of *X* for $100, receives a $50 dividend 20 days later and sells the stock for $50 the next day. What is *Y*'s taxable income from the dividend and the stock sale?

Alternative: *Y* buys all the stock of *X* for $100 and causes *X* to pay a $50 dividend 10 days later and sells the stock for $50 six months later.

Organization of a Corporation: Section 351 and Related Problems

3A   Requirements of § 351 Nonrecognition

SUBJECT: The property requirement—Introduction to consequences of debt cancellation—Identifying the "control club"—The meaning of "immediately after"—Introduction to the step transaction doctrine

ASSIGNMENT

B&E: ¶¶ 3.01, 3.02, 3.03, 3.07–3.09, 3.12[1], 3.12[2], 3.12[4], 3.12[5], 3.15[1], 5.06[1], 5.07

Code: §§ 83(a), 83(h), 317(a), 351, 368(c), 1001, 1012, 1031(a)(2)(B), 1032

Regs: §§ 1.61-6, 1.351-1, 1.1001-1(a), 1.1002-1, 1.1032-1, 1.1361-1(*l*)(1)

Cases: Caruth v. US, 688 F. Supp. 1129 (DC Tex. 1988) (ignore Part II; why did the taxpayer transfer the stock to his corporation?), aff'd on other grounds

Other materials: Rev. Rul. 59-259, 1959-2 CB 115; Rev. Rul. 84-111, 1984-2 CB 88; Rev. Proc. 2003-3, § 3.01(30), or current "no-ruling Revenue Procedure" [*Note:* This revenue procedure should be reviewed for applicability to all lessons, even though it will not be repeated in each assignment.]

PROBLEMS

(1)   *A* wants to transfer land worth $100 with a $50 basis to *X* for $100 in value. How much income will *A* realize and recognize if *A* receives $100 cash from *X*, and what will be *X*'s basis in the land? Does *A*'s income recognition change if *X* transfers its own stock to *A* in the exchange (assume the "general rule" applies)? Will the answer change in the stock case if *A* is the sole shareholder of *X*; conceptually, why should it change?

(2)   *A* contributes property to *X*, a newly formed corporation, in exchange for 75 shares. As part of the same transaction, *B* contributes services to *X* in exchange for 25 shares. Does § 351 apply to the contributions of *A* and *B*?

(3)   *A* contributes to *X*, a newly formed corporation, property worth $80 with a basis of $60 in exchange for 20 shares. Assume the stock is worth $1 per share. As part of the same transaction, *B* (an employee of *A*) contributes to *X* property worth $20 with a basis of $10 in exchange for 80 shares. How much income must *A* and *B* recognize (assume that if § 351 applies, *A*'s basis in the stock *A* receives is the same as *A*'s basis in the property)?

(4)   *A* owns all 90 shares of Class A voting common stock and all 90 shares of Class C nonvoting common stock of *X*. *B* owns all 10 shares of Class B voting common stock and all 10 shares of Class D nonvoting common stock of *X*. Does *A* control *X* under § 368(c)? Can *X* make an S election? What if the charter of *X* is amended so that Class D shares have 1/10 vote per share?

ADD TO ASSIGNMENT

B&E: ¶¶ 3.04, 3.12[3], 4.25

Code: §§ 61(a)(12), 108(e)(2), 108(e)(6), 108(e)(8), 267(a)(1), 1222(3), 1271(a)(1), 1275(a)(1)(A)

Regs: § 1.61-12(a)

Other materials: Rev. Rul. 64-56, 1964-1 CB 133

(5)   *A* and *X* are both accrual-method taxpayers. *A* owns all the stock of *X*. *A* supplied services to *X* and accrued income therefor (represented by bookkeeping entries of accounts receivable and payable) of $10; *X* deducted $10. Later, *A* forgave the account owing in return for stock of *X* worth $6. How much income or loss must *A* and *X* recognize? What would result if *X* were on the cash method and had not deducted the $10?

(6)   *A* is an inventor who contributes a nonexclusive license to use his new patented invention to his wholly owned corporation *X* for 100 shares of stock. Does § 351 apply?

ADD TO ASSIGNMENT

Regs: § 1.351-1(a)(3)

Cases: American Bantam Car Co., 11 TC 397 (1948), aff'd per curiam, 177 F2d 513 (3d Cir. 1949), cert. denied, 339 US 920 (1950) (did taxpayer want § 351 to apply?); West Coast Marketing Corp., 46 TC 32 (1966)

Other materials: Rev. Rul. 79-194, 1979-1 CB 145; Rev. Rul. 78-294, 1978-2 CB 141; Rev. Rul. 2003-51, 2003-21 IRB 938

(7)   *A* contributes appreciated property worth $80, with an adjusted basis of $60, to newly formed *X* and in exchange for all of the 80 outstanding shares of *X*. Immediately thereafter, *A* gives 20 shares to *B*, *A*'s employee, in payment of accrued wages. Does § 351(a) apply to *A*'s exchange of property for stock? How much gross income must *A* and *B* recognize, if any?

(8)   *A* owns all the stock of *X*, which is worth $1,000. *X* wants to acquire land worth $75 (*A/B* $100) from *B*. *A* proposes to transfer $1 of cash to *X* at the same time *B* transfers the land to *X* for stock. Will *B* recognize loss on the transfer of the depreciated land?

ADD TO ASSIGNMENT

B&E: ¶ 3.19

Code: § 1014

Other materials: Rev. Rul. 84-71, 1984-1 CB 106

(9)   *A* owns 20 percent of *T*'s stock, which is highly appreciated. *A* does not want
to sell. The remaining 80 percent of *T*'s stock is publicly held. *X* wants to
acquire at least 80 percent of *T*'s stock for cash but knows it cannot get that
much stock in a tender offer. How can *A* and *X* use § 351 to cash out the
public and satisfy *A*'s desires? Why does *A* not want to sell? [*Hint: A* is age
77.]

3B   Boot; Basis; Debt; "Midstream" Issues

SUBJECT: Basis, gain recognition, and holding-period consequences of passing and
flunking § 351(a)—Creation of the corporate "lobster pot"—Contributions to capital—
Boot—Debt into and from a corporation—Incorporation of an ongoing business

ASSIGNMENT

B&E: ¶¶ 3.05, 3.10[1], 3.10[2], 3.10[4], 3.11[1], 3.11[2], 3.11[4], 3.11[5], 3.11[6],
3.12[5], 3.13, 3.14

Code: §§ 118, 267(a)(1), 351, 358, 362(a), 362(c), 1012, 1016(a)(1), 1221(1), 1222(3),
1223(1), 1223(2), 7701(a)(42), 7701(a)(43), 7701(a)(44)

Regs: §§ 1.118-1, 1.351-2, 1.351-3, 1.358-1, 1.358-2(b), 1.362-1(a)

Cases: CIR v. Fink, 483 US 89 (1987)

Other materials: Rev. Rul. 74-503, 1974-2 CB 117; Rev. Rul. 84-111, 1984-2 CB 88;
Rev. Rul. 2003-51, 2003-21 IRB 938

PROBLEMS

Assumptions: Except as otherwise stated, *A* starts out with nondepreciable real property (a capital asset) worth $100 (adjusted basis $40) and ends up with cash of $50 plus a 50 percent interest (worth $50) in *X*, a newly organized corporation that owns the property.

In each problem, determine the following:

1.   *A*'s amount realized

2.   *A*'s gain or loss realized

3.   *A*'s gain or loss recognized and the character thereof

4.   *A*'s basis in the *X* stock received

5.   *A*'s holding period for the *X* stock received (tacked or not?)

6.   *X*'s basis in the property received

7.   *X*'s holding period for the property received (tacked or not?)

8.   The amount and character of *X*'s gain if *X* immediately sells the property for $100

(1)   *A* transfers the property to *X* in exchange for all of *X*'s stock. Shortly thereafter, *A* sells half of his *X* stock to *B* for $50 and either

(a)   The stock sale is a "separate" event from the prior incorporation transaction; or

(b)   The stock sale is an integral part of the incorporation plan.

Would the results be different if *X* made an S election? What if the basis for *A*'s property were $200 rather than $40?

(2) *A* sells a half interest in the property to *B* for $50. *A* and *B* then jointly transfer their property interests to *X* in exchange for *X*'s stock.

(3) *A* and *B* jointly organize *X*. *A* transfers his property to *X* in exchange for $50 in cash and half of *X*'s stock. *B* transfers $50 in cash to *X* in exchange for the other half of *X*'s stock.

ADD TO ASSIGNMENT

B&E: ¶¶ 3.05[3], 3.05[4]

Code: §§ 351(g), 453(a)–453(c), 453(f), 453(g), 453(k)

(4) What would result in (3) above if *A* received $50 in five-year notes instead of cash? Assume the notes are debt and not equity.

(5) What would result in (1)(a) above if *A* receives only "pure preferred" stock of *X* that is required to be redeemed in five years for $100?

ADD TO ASSIGNMENT

B&E: ¶¶ 3.06, 3.10[3], 311[3], 3.16–3.18, 8.05[7]

Code: §§ 357, 358(d)(1), 362(d)

Regs: §§ 1.357-1, 1.357-2, 1.358-3, 1.1001-2(a)(4)

Cases: US v. Hendler, 303 US 564 (1938)

Other materials: Rev. Rul. 80-198, 1980-2 CB 113; Rev. Rul. 95-74, 1995-2 CB 36

(6) *A* borrows $50 from *L* (nonrecourse) on the security of the property. Shortly thereafter, *A* transfers the property to *X* (subject to this debt) in exchange for half of *X*'s stock, and *B* transfers $50 in cash to *X* in exchange for the other half of *X*'s stock. *X* subsequently uses the $50 cash to repay *L*.

(7)   Same as (6) but the debt is recourse as to A and X does not assume it and A receives 100 shares and B receives 50 shares.

(8) A transfers $100 in uncollected customer accounts receivable (from A's cash-basis service business) to X in exchange for half of X's common stock plus X's assumption of $50 of accounts payable attributable to the service business (which $50 A could have deducted upon payment in cash). B transfers $50 in cash to X in exchange for the other half of X's stock. X uses this cash to pay off the assumed accounts payable. Variation: A transfers the receivables but not the payables to X (and vice versa).

ADD TO ASSIGNMENT

Cases: Lessinger v. CIR, 872 F2d 519 (2d Cir. 1989); Peracchi v. CIR, 143 F3d 487 (9th Cir. 1998)

(9)   Same as (6), but A also contributes A's note for $10 to X. Also, apply this alternative to question (7), but assume that X assumes the liability.

Corporation's Capital Structure: Debt Versus Equity

Note: This lesson may be skipped at this point and assigned after Lesson 8 on liquidations, because it can serve there as a review. In addition, this lesson involves in part the consequences of distributions and of termination of the enterprise, which may be understood better at the later time. Alternatively, problem (5) alone can be deferred, as it is more advanced. Reduction of the top rate on dividends to 15 percent in 2003 (the same as the reduced rate on capital gains) will also have a major impact on the issues raised in this Lesson.

SUBJECT: Classification of corporate debt and equity—Examination of possible legislative "integration" of the corporate and individual income taxes—Do-it-yourself integration—Cradle-to-grave review of consequences of different methods of capitalizing a corporation—Basis of debt and equity held by S corporation shareholders

ASSIGNMENT

B&E: ¶ 1.08

Code: §§ 1(h)(11), 163(a)

PROBLEMS

(1) X has an annual net operating income of $1.5 million, 99,000 shares of stock outstanding, and no debt. X pays federal income tax of $510,000 ($1.5 million multiplied by 34 percent), resulting in net after-tax income of $990,000 ($1.5 million less $510,000). Earnings per share are $10 ($990,000 divided by 99,000 shares). The stock sells on the market at about $80 per share (or 8 times earnings).

Y tenders for and acquires all of the outstanding *X* stock for $120 cash per share, 50 percent more than the market price, for a total price of $11.88 million. *Y* puts up $880,000 of its own funds and raises the remaining $11 million by issuing balloon notes paying 12 percent interest only for 10 years, to be assumed by *X*. The annual net operating income of *X* after the buyout is unchanged, except for debt service and taxes.

Complete the following chart showing the distribution of ownership of *X*'s operating income before and after the leveraged buyout, using a 34 percent corporate tax rate:

	Before	*After*
X's original shareholders	$ 990,000	-0-
Bondholders	-0-	$_____
Y	-0-	$_____
Corporate income taxes	$ 510,000	$_____
Total operating income	$1,500,000	$1,500,000

Who has benefited from this transaction: the public sector or the private sector?

ADD TO ASSIGNMENT

B&E: ¶¶ 4.01–4.03

Code: § 385; scan §§ 163(a), 163(f), 163(j), 163(*l*), and 279

Cases: Paulsen v. CIR, 469 US 131 (1985)

(2)   *X* has 10 shareholders, each of whom owns 100 of its 1,000 outstanding shares of common stock (worth $100 per share). No other stock is outstanding. Determine whether the securities described in the situations below are debt or equity of *X*.

   (a)   *X* issues a secured standard form note to the bank promising unconditionally to repay in five years $1 million borrowed, plus interest at the bank's prime plus one percent.

(b)   *X* issues to the public for cash $1 million worth of "pure preferred" stock (nonvoting, nonparticipating, nonconvertible), callable in five years at par, paying an 18 percent cumulative dividend. Would it matter if the stock were callable below par or had a declining dividend?

(c)   In return for a transfer of $1 million, *X* issues an unsecured promissory note for $1 million to Mr. Jones, well-known local venture capitalist, payable in 10 years with interest keyed to *X*'s profitability. The note is subordinated to all other debt. *X* could not have borrowed this amount on these terms from a bank.

(d)   *X* issues to the public 1,000 notes for $1,000 each, maturing in 20 years, at which time the holder will be entitled to elect to receive either $600 cash or 50 shares of *X* common stock. *X* can call the notes for $600 after two years, but, upon call, the holder can convert to 50 shares of stock. Interest will be paid quarterly in an amount based on *X*'s common dividend, but not less than $60 per annum. The interest rate for nonconvertible unsubordinated debt in the market is 12 percent. The notes will be subordinated to all other debt.

(e)   *X* issues to the public $1 million in subordinated unsecured "junk bonds," paying deferred interest resulting in an 18 percent yield to maturity, with all payments of principal and interest due in installments payable from the sixth to the fifteenth year.

ADD TO ASSIGNMENT

B&E: ¶¶ 4.04, 6.02[3], 6.06[4]

Code: §§ 1361(c)(5), 1366(d)(1), 1367(b)(2), 1368(b)(1)

Regs: § 1.1361-1(*l*)(4)(ii)

Cases: Fin Hay Realty Co. v. US, 398 F2d 694 (3d Cir. 1968)

(3) X issues an unsecured standard form note to each of its shareholders promising to repay, in five years, $100,000 loaned plus interest at the Bank of America prime plus one percent. X could not have borrowed this amount on these terms from a bank.

(4)   List the considerations that uniquely apply to an S corporation shareholder's decision whether to capitalize the corporation with a stock purchase or a loan from the shareholder to the corporation, or a loan from a third party.

ADVANCED ASSIGNMENT

B&E: Chapter 4, Part B (scan Part C)

Code: §§ 165(g), 166, 351, 358, 362(a), 453, 453B(a), 1239

(5) A owns undeveloped land (a capital asset, basis of $40, value $100), which A contributes to X, a newly created corporation, in exchange for the alternative consideration in (a) through (e) below. Assume no OID in any debt. With respect to each situation in (a) through (e) below, answer the following questions:

    1.   What are the income recognition and basis consequences to A and X on the exchange?

    2.   What are the income and deduction consequences to A and X while the securities are outstanding and upon their repayment or redemption by X?

    3.   What are the income and deduction consequences to A and X if X subsequently becomes insolvent and A's entire investment becomes worthless before any repayment (other than dividends or interest) is made?

    4.   Could X make an S election, and how would that change the results in questions 1 through 3 above?

5.   What results in questions 1 through 3 above would change if *A* were a corporation?

(a)   20 shares of common stock (FMV $20) and 80 shares of $1 preferred stock paying 8 percent cumulative dividends.

(b)   20 shares of common stock (FMV $20) and $80 principal amount (and FMV) of 20-year, registered bonds paying half the principal after 10 years and the rest at maturity (with 8 percent interest payable annually). *A* reports the principal payments on the bonds under § 453.

(c)   Same as (b) above, except the payment of the bonds cannot be reported under § 453, because *A* contributed depreciable property instead of raw land and § 453(g)(2) is not applicable.

(d)   Same as (b) above, except that *A* already owned the 20 shares (acquired for $20 cash) of *X* common stock and transfers the land for $100 in bonds in a "separate" transaction.

(e)   20 shares of common stock (worth $80) and warrants for *X* stock (worth $20).

Dividends and Other
Nonliquidating Distributions

5A   General

SUBJECT: Function and determination of E&P—Taxation of shareholders on corporate distributions not in exchange for stock [*Note*: By reducing the top rate on dividends to 15 percent (the same as capital gains), 2003 legislation has significantly changed the tax stakes in this Lesson.]

ASSIGNMENT

B&E: ¶¶ 8.01, 8.02

Code: §§ 1(h)(11), 61(a)(7), 301(a)–301(d), 316(a), 317(a)

Regs: §§ 1.301-1(a), 1.301-1(c), 1.301-1(f), Ex (1), 1.301-1(m)

PROBLEMS

(1)   *A* owns all of the stock of *X*. The stock's basis is $100. *X* has a total of current and accumulated earnings and profits of $50. *X* distributes $200 cash to *A* "with respect to his stock" (i.e., as a state law "dividend"). How is the $200 taxed? What is *A*'s stock basis after the distribution? Alternatively, *X* distributes to *A A*'s note to *X* for $200 borrowed from *X*.

ADD TO ASSIGNMENT

B&E: ¶¶ 8.03–8.04

Code: §§ 275(a)(1), 312(a)(1), 312(a)(2), 312(f)(1), 312(k)(1)

Regs: §§ 1.312-6, 1.316-1(a)(1), 1.316-1(a)(2), 1.316-1(e), Ex. (1), 1.316-2(a), 1.316-2(b), 1.317-1

PROBLEMS

Assumptions: The stock of X is owned equally by two shareholders: Y (a corporation) and A (an individual). X and Y use the accrual method, A uses the cash method, and all use a calendar taxable year. Assume § 1059 does not apply. Use a 34 percent corporate tax rate in this problem. During the current year, X accrued income and expenses as follows:

Gross income from business	$500
Dividends on AT&T stock (consider § 243)	100
Interest on municipal bonds (§ 103)	100
Capital gain	100
Total	$800
Deductible § 162(a)(1) business expenses	$430
Noncapital expenses not deductible under § 162(e)	90
Capital losses (see § 1211(a))	146
Total	$666
Net	$134

(2)   On December 24 of the preceding year, Y and A incorporated X and capitalized X with cash of $100 each. On December 31 of that preceding year, Y and A received distributions from X of $5 each; X did not earn any income for that year. In addition, Y and A received distributions of $5 each, in the current year. Which distributions should be gross income to Y and A, in what amounts, and why? What does E&P have to do with this?

24

Alternative: A just bought the *X* shares on December 30 of the current year from another shareholder for FMV of $145, before the declaration and payment of a $5 distribution to *A* on December 31 of the current year. Should the distribution be taxable income to *A*? Why?

(3)   Now assume that *Y*'s basis in its *X* stock is $100 and *A*'s basis in his *X* stock is $40. On January 2 of the current taxable year, *X* distributes $100 in cash to *Y* and $100 in cash to *A*. As of the end of the preceding taxable year, *X*'s accumulated E&P was zero. What are the tax consequences of this distribution to *X*, *Y*, and *A*? [*Hint*: First compute *X*'s current-year taxable income and then compute current-year E&P before reducing the E&P for the distribution ("interim E&P"); after reducing for the distribution, compute final accumulated E&P.]

Variation: How much dividend would *Y* and the holders of *A*'s shares receive if *A*'s shares were owned by a different shareholder every quarter and $50 was distributed ratably to all shareholders quarterly?

(4)   Suppose under the basic facts in (3) above that *X* had an accumulated deficit of $100 in its E&P account as of December 31 of the preceding taxable year.

ADD TO ASSIGNMENT

B&E: ¶ 8.07[1]

Code: § 312(d)

Regs: §§ 1.61-9(c), 1.301-1(b), 1.451-1(a), 1.451-2(b), 1.6042-2(b)

Cases: Caruth Corp. v. US, 864 F2d 644 (5th Cir. 1989)

(5)   How would your answer to (3) above change if, on December 1 of the current year (the declaration date), *X*'s board of directors voted to pay the $200 distribution by mailing the checks on December 31 of the current taxable year (the payment date, the identification of which is a practice generally used only

by widely held corporations) to shareholders of record on December 15 of the current taxable year (the record date), such checks actually being received by *Y* and *A* in the mail on January 2 of the next year? Assume that *Y* and *A* are the public and that they are the only shareholders (as in the basic facts).

(6)   Who recognizes how much income and of what kind in (5) above if *A* sells his *X* stock to *C* for $540 (assume FMV) on December 10 of the current taxable year?

Alternative: What if *Y* sells its stock to *Z* on December 20 for $440?

ADD TO ASSIGNMENT

B&E: ¶ 8.07[2]

Regs: § 1.301-1(*l*)

Cases: Litton Indus., 89 TC 1086 (1987) (acq.)

(7)   *A* owns all of the stock of *X*, with a basis of $1 million. *X* owns $1 million cash and a hotel. *X* has $1 million of E&P. *B* wants to buy the stock of *X* for $5M after *X* has distributed the cash, but will pay $6 million for the stock without a prior distribution to *A*. What should *A* want, and why?

(8)   Change (7) so that the owner of *X* is not *A* but another corporation, *Y*. What should *Y* want, and why?

ADD TO ASSIGNMENT

B&E: ¶¶ 6.04, 6.06, 6.07, 6.08

Code: §§ 1362(d)(3), 1366(a), 1366(b), 1366(c), 1366(d)(1), 1367(a), 1368, 1371(c)(1), 1374(a), 1374(c)(1), 1375(a), 1375(b), 1377(a)

(9)   Suppose that Y is an individual and that X has always been an S corporation. What is X's E&P? How is each shareholder's personal income tax return affected for the current year by the tax items of X? How will X's distribution of $100 to each shareholder in the current year affect shareholders?

Alternative: X has E&P of $100 from years before it was an S corporation and nothing in its accumulated adjustments account from prior S years. The $100 capital gain is from the sale of stock held for investment, and the $500 gross income from business is also gross receipts from business.

5B   Distributions in Kind and Constructive Distributions

SUBJECT: *General Utilities* repeal—Effect on E&P—Debt distributions and OID—Disguised distributions [*Note*: The latter issue has been greatly eased by 2003 legislation taxing dividends at the same rate as capital gains (generally 15 percent).]

ASSIGNMENT

B&E: ¶¶ 8.20–8.22

Code: §§ 61(a)(3), 301(a)–301(c), 311, 312(a)–312(c), 316(a), 317(a), 337(d)(1), 1001, 1222(3)

Regs: §§ 1.301-1(g), 1.312-3

Cases: General Utils. & Operating Co. v. Helvering, 296 US 200 (1935)

PROBLEMS

Assumptions for problems (1) through (10): A owns half the common stock of X with an adjusted basis of $40, and Y owns the other half of the X common stock with an adjusted basis of $100. X's current E&P from current-year income and expenses/losses (before consideration of the events described in (1) through (10) below) is $94, and X has no accumulated E&P. X uses the accrual method, all taxpayers are on the calendar year, and § 1059 does not apply. Assume that the corporate tax rate is 34 percent. [*Hint:* First derive an "interim" E&P based on the events described in each problem, but not including the downward adjustment for the distribution itself.]

(1) *X* distributes, in kind, its long-held AT&T stock with an adjusted basis of $40 and FMV of $100 to *Y*; *X* also distributes other long-held AT&T shares with an adjusted basis of $60 and FMV of $100 to *A*. What are the results to *A*, *Y*, and *X*?

Alternative: The basis of the stock distributed to *A* is $120.

(2) Suppose that each block of AT&T stock in the basic facts of (1) above was subject to a $50 non-recourse liability or, alternatively, a $120 non-recourse liability.

ADD TO ASSIGNMENT

Code: §§ 301(e), 312(n)(5), 453B(a)

(3) Suppose that the distributed properties were § 453 "installment obligations" of *C*.

ADD TO ASSIGNMENT

B&E: ¶¶ 4.21[1], 8.23

Regs: § 1.301-1(*l*)

(4) Assume for this problem that beginning E&P is $100, rather than $94. *X* issues and distributes two negotiable notes payable by *X* to *A* and *Y* (each note having a face amount and "stated principal amount" and "stated redemption price at maturity" of $120 and FMV of $100). What would result now, during the terms of the notes, and upon collection? First, ignore OID, market discount, and the time-value-of-money rules generally.

LESSON 5

[This problem can be used as a means of introducing/reviewing the original issue discount rules, in which case add to the assignment: B&E ¶¶ 4.40, 4.41, 4.42, 4.44; Code §§ 163(e)(1), 1271(a)(1), 1272(a)(1), 1273(a), 1273(b), 1274(a), 1274(c)(1), 1275(a)(1)(A), 1275(a)(4), 1276(a)(1), 1278(a)(1)(C)(i), 1278(a)(1)(c)(ii); and answer this question: Now apply OID rules as if the notes were publicly traded and bore "adequate stated interest." Next, assume "adequate stated interest," but assume that the notes were not publicly traded.]

ADD TO ASSIGNMENT

B&E: ¶ 8.05

Code: §§ 1(h)(11), 83(a), 83(h), 162(a)(1), 7872(a)–7872(c)

Regs: §§ 1.118-1, 1.162-8, 1.301-1(j), 1.301-1(*l*), 1.301-1(m), 1.312-1(d), 1.1032-1(a)

Cases: Alterman Foods, Inc. v. US, 611 F2d 866 (Cl. Ct. 1979)

(5)   *X* leases some rental property that it owns to *T*, and *T* agrees to pay the annual rent of $60 directly to *X*'s shareholders, *A* and *Y*.

(6)   *X* sells an apartment building that it owns to *A* and *Y* jointly for $100. The property has a basis of $100 and a value of $200.

   Alternative: A and *Y* paid $300 for the property.

(7)   *X* transfers property (a capital asset) with a basis of $20 and a value of $100 to *A* as "salary" (Hint: see *Fender Sales*).

   Alternative: X paid *A*'s "salary" with its preferred stock (worth $100).

(8)   *A* is the sole shareholder of *X*, which advanced cash to *A* from time to time over a period of years upon an open account maintained on the corporate ledger as "A/R shdr." The amount now totals $100,000, including interest at 6 percent, which the bookkeeper has accrued annually. No repayments have been made. Are there any tax consequences to *A* or *X*?

ADD TO ASSIGNMENT

B&E: ¶¶ 6.06, 6.07, 6.08

Code: §§ 1366(a)–1366(d)(1), 1367(a), 1374 (scan), 1368, 1371(a)

(9)   Answer (1) above assuming that X has always been an S corporation (which means Y is an individual and X has no E&P) and has no other income or deduction item for the current year. Would your answer change if this were X's first year as an S corporation year and X had $100 E&P from prior years as a C corporation?

(10)   Continuing with the basic facts in (9) above, the next year, X has non-separately computed loss from operations of $100, no other tax items, and zero net worth when X borrows $100 from Bank upon the strength of A's personal guaranty.

ADVANCED ASSIGNMENT

Code: § 1234(a)

(11) X is a publicly owned operating company that holds as an investment 10,000 shares (basis $40,000 and FMV $100,000) of the common stock of Y, also a public company. X distributes pro rata to its shareholders rights to purchase Y shares from X at $10 per share at any time during the next two years. By the end of the two-year period, the market price of Y stock has increased to $15 per share. Some rights holders exercised them and others sold them in the market to third parties who exercised them. All rights had been exercised by the expiration date. What are the tax results to X and to X's shareholders?

Alternative: What if the rights lapsed unexercised?

Stock Redemptions and Partial Liquidations

6A   General

SUBJECT: Overview of effects of redemptions on shareholders and corporations—Attribution rules—Redemptions that are sales or exchanges because they are disproportionate or not essentially equivalent to a dividend (NEED) [*Note:* The attribution rules are not introduced until the next addition to the Assignment, but since some of the authorities assigned below rely on those rules, the attribution concept should be introduced generally. However, 2003 legislation (under which dividends are taxed at the same rate as capital gains, a top rate of 15 percent) has greatly reduced the importance of this problem.]

ASSIGNMENT

B&E: ¶¶ 9.01, 9.02[1], 9.03, 9.05, 9.20, 9.21, 9.22

Code: §§ 1(h)(11), 61(a)(3), 61(a)(7), 267(a)–267(c), 302(a), 302(b), 302(d), 312(a), 312(n)(7), 317(b), 1059(d)(6), 1059(e)(1)

Regs: §§ 1.61-6(a), 1.302-1(a), 1.302-2, 1.302-3, 1.1012-1(c)(1)–1.1012-1(c)(2)

Prop. Regs: § 1.302-5 (anti-basis-shift rules)

Cases: US v. Davis, 397 US 301 (1970); Rogers v. US, 281 F3d 1108 (10th Cir. 2002)

Other materials: Rev. Rul. 75-502, 1975-2 CB 111; Rev. Rul. 76-364, 1976-2 CB 91; Rev. Rul. 77-426, 1977-2 CB 87; Rev. Rul. 78-401, 1978-2 CB 127; Rev. Rul. 81-289, 1981-2 CB 82; Rev. Rul. 85-106, 1985-2 CB 116

PROBLEMS

Assumptions: X is owned entirely by two individuals, A and B (who are unrelated unless otherwise stated). A owns 60 shares of X common stock (bought in one transaction for $600). B owns 40 shares of X common stock (with a basis of $30 per share). The stock's FMV is $20 per share. X's E&P is $500; X uses the accrual method of accounting. What are the results to the parties from the alternative transactions in (1) through (9) below (i.e., the amount and character of shareholder income or loss and the E&P impact)?

(1) A sells 10 X shares to B for $200. Alternatively, what should A do if 50 of A's shares have a $10 per share basis and the other 10 shares have a $20 per share basis? Are there any circumstances in which this sale could be a redemption?

(2) A sells 30 shares back to X for $600.

(3) A sells 20 shares back to X for $400.

(4)   What would result to B if X redeems 10 of B's shares for $200? What is the minimum number of shares that B must have redeemed to ensure sale or exchange treatment?

(5) A sells 10 shares back to X for $200.

   Alternative: A is a corporation.

ADD TO ASSIGNMENT

B&E: ¶ 9.02

Code: § 318

Regs: §§ 1.318-1, 1.318-2, 1.318-3, 1.318-4

Cases: Zenz v. Quinlivan, 213 F2d 914 (6th Cir. 1954); Merrill Lynch Co., 120 TC 12 (2003)

LESSON 6

Other materials: Rev. Rul. 85-14, 1985-1 CB 92; Rev. Rul. 89-64, 1989-1 CB 91

(6) *A* sells 30 shares back to *X* for $600. Shortly thereafter, *B* sells 10 shares back to *X* for $200 in an exchange that had been agreed to in the preceding year. What would result to *B*? What would result to *A* if *B* sold 11 shares, rather than 10?

(7) In one transaction, *A* sells 20 *X* shares to *B* for $400 and 10 shares back to *X* for $200.

(8) *A* sells 30 shares back to *X* for $600. What would result if *A* and *B* are "related" in the following alternative ways:

(a) *B* is *A*'s brother, and their father is living.

(b) *B* is *A*'s equal partner in a two-person partnership.

Alternative: The partnership owns an option to purchase *B*'s shares in *X*.

(c) *B* is a corporation in which *A* owns one half of the stock.

Alternatives:

(i) *A* owns 45 percent of the stock.

(ii) *A* owns 45 percent of the stock and *C*, *A*'s father, owns 5 percent of the outstanding *B* shares.

(iii) *A* owns 45 percent of the stock and *B* is an S corporation.

(d) *A* is a trust of which *B* is the sole income beneficiary for *B*'s life. Query: Would *A*'s shares be attributed to *B*? Could *X* be an S corporation?

(e) *A* has an option to buy *B*'s shares.

33

Alternative: B has an option to buy 21 shares from *X*.

(9)   If *A* and *B* each own 50 shares, rather than 60 shares and 40 shares, respectively, how many shares will *A* and *B* each own by attribution? Assume no relationships other than as shareholders.

6B Termination of Interest; Partial Liquidations; Related Matters

SUBJECT: The third and fourth routes to stock sale treatment—Greenmail—Bootstrap redemptions (LBOs)—STD applications generally—*GU* repeal avoidance efforts [*Note:* More on *GU* in Lesson 8: Complete Liquidations]

ASSIGNMENT

B&E: Primary: ¶ 9.04; Secondary: ¶¶ 5.04[6], 8.21[4], 9.25

Code: Primary: §§ 302(b)(3), 302(c), 318; Ancillary: §§ 162(k), 267(a)(1), 337(d), 453(k)(2)(A), 1001

Regs: §§ 1.302-2(c), 1.302-4

PROBLEMS

(1)   *A* owns 60 of the 100 outstanding *X* shares, with a $600 adjusted basis. *B* owns the other 40 shares. If *A* wants to sell a few shares and avoid distribution treatment, will *A* want to sell to *B* or to *X*? How will *B* feel about *A*'s choice? Will *A*'s and *B*'s concerns change if *X* is an S corporation with no E&P account?

(2)   *A* owns 60 shares ($10 per share basis) and *B* owns 40 shares ($30 per share basis) of *X*, representing all of *X*'s outstanding shares. *A* and *B* are unrelated unless otherwise stated. *X* has $500 E&P. What are the results to *A*, *B*, and *X* from the following alternative transactions?

(a)   *A* sells all of *A*'s *X* stock to *B* for $200 in cash and $1,000 in notes payable over a 10-year period.

(b)   *X* redeems (but does not cancel) all of *A*'s stock on the same terms as (a) above. Is this an LBO? What if *A* stayed on as *X*'s president with compensation tied to *X*'s profits? What if *A* were a "corporate raider"?

(c)   Suppose in (a) and (b) above that *A*'s stock is sold or redeemed at fair market value for $200 cash plus an $800 note (face and FMV), rather than a $1,000 note. *A* is *B*'s father. After the sale, *A* moves to Florida and has no connection with *X* whatsoever. Alternatively, what if *A* stays in town and "consults" with *X*, maintaining the same office at *X* and receiving $2,000 per month plus medical and life insurance benefits? What if *B* hates *A*, and the feeling is reciprocated?

ADD TO ASSIGNMENT

B&E: ¶¶ 9.06, 9.23, 9.24[1], 9.24[2], 9.24[3]

Code: §§ 311, 1060, 5881 (scan)

Regs: §§ 1.1060-1(b)(3), Ex. (3), 1.1041-2 (2003)

Cases: Zenz v. Quinlivan, 213 F2d 914 (6th Cir. 1954); Estate of James Durkin, 99 TC 561 (1992); Carol Read, 114 TC 14 (2000); Merrill Lynch Co., 120 TC 12 (2003)

Other materials: Rev. Rul. 69-608, 1969-2 CB 42

(d)   Suppose in (a) above that *X* pays off *B*'s note as payments fall due. Is this a smart way to do an LBO? What if *B* is a corporation that recently acquired its *X* stock?

(e)   Suppose in (b) above that *B* had the option to buy *A*'s *X* stock at $20 per share, but instead allowed *X* to make the purchase.

(f)   Suppose in (a) above that after the contract had been signed, but before closing, B assigned the agreement to X, B was released (with the consent of A), and X completed the transaction. What if B is a corporation that recently acquired its 40 percent by a market tender?

(g) A sells 10 of A's shares to B for $200 in cash and, as part of the "same transaction," sells the balance of the shares to X for $1,000 in notes payable over 10 years. Will A do this if it is a corporation?

(h)   Suppose in (g) above that instead of paying for A's stock with the notes, X distributed land worth $1,000 (basis $200) to A in exchange for the 50 shares of X stock.

ADD TO ASSIGNMENT

Code: §§ 1367(a), 1368, 1371(a), 1377(a)

(3)   In (2)(h) above, what if X is an S corporation but has no E&P? Assume § 1374 does not apply. Does it matter when during the year A's stock sales to B and X occur?

ADD TO ASSIGNMENT

B&E: ¶ 9.07

Code: §§ 302(b)(4), 302(e), 346

Regs: § 1.346-1

(4) A and B own X, which owns Y and Z, each of which operates a substantial and active business. X wants to dispose of Z's business, either by a sale of Z stock or of Z's business, and A and B would like to receive the net sale proceeds and not be taxed as upon a dividend. Can and how can these desires be accomplished?

6C   Redemptions by Affiliated Corporations

SUBJECT: Determining when a shareholder's sale of stock to a corporate buyer other than the issuer may be treated as a redemption—Consequences of such treatment [*Note:* Dividend consequences have been greatly reduced by 2003 legislation under which dividends are taxed at the same rate as capital gains (with a top rate of 15 percent for both).]

Note: This subject is addressed again in Lesson 11C.

ASSIGNMENT

B&E: ¶¶ 9.09, 9.24[4]

Code: Primary: §§ 1(h)(11), 304, 1059(e)(1)(A); Secondary: §§ 301(a)–301(d), 302, 317, 318, 351, 362, 1001, 1012

Regs: §§ 1.302-2(c), 1.304-1, 1.304-2, 1.304-3 [be aware that parts of §§ 1.304-2 and 1.304-3 are seriously out of date and are in conflict with the statute], 1.304-5, 1.318-1(b)(1)

Prop. Regs: §§ 1.304-2(a), 1.304-2(c) (2002)

Fill in the chart that appears at the end of the problems, both generically and for the problems.

PROBLEMS

Assumptions: X, Y, and *Z,* although in different businesses, have the following identical characteristics: (1) cash of $100; (2) other assets with a basis of $100 and FMV of $300; (3) no liabilities; (4) E&P of $100; and (5) capital stock outstanding of 100 shares common. Each share of stock of each corporation is worth $4.

In each of the following situations, determine the tax effects on the shareholders and the corporations, including stock and asset basis.

STUDY PROBLEMS

(1)   *A* owns all of the outstanding *X* stock with a basis of $200. *A* owns 45 shares of the 100 outstanding shares of *Y* with a basis of $90. *B* owns 55 *Y* shares with a basis of $110. *A* sells all of the *X* stock to *Y* for $400 cash and notes.

Alternatives:

(a)   *A* and *B* each own 50 shares of *Y* stock with a basis of $100 each.

(b)   *A* owns 51 percent of *Y* stock with a basis of $100.

Alternative: A is a corporation that has owned the *X* stock for 10 years, but not during the entire period of *X*'s existence.

ADD TO ASSIGNMENT

Prop. Regs: § 1.304-2(c), Ex. (4) (2002)

Cases: Coyle v. US, 415 F2d 488 (4th Cir. 1968); Merrill Lynch Co., 120 TC 12 (2003)

Other materials: Rev. Rul. 70-496, 1970-2 CB 74

(2)   *A* owns all of the *X* stock with a basis of $200. *A*'s three sons own all of the *Y* stock equally. *A* sells one half of the *X* stock to *Y* for $200.

Alternative: *A* sells all of the *X* stock to *Y* for $400 cash and notes, and *X* has $200 E&P, instead of $100.

ADD TO ASSIGNMENT

Regs: § 1.304-4T

Other materials: Rev. Rul. 74-605, 1974-2 CB 97

(3)   *X* owns all of the *Y* stock with a basis of $200. *Y* owns all of the *Z* stock with a basis of $100. *Y* sells its *Z* stock to *X* for $400.

(4) X owns all of the Y stock with a basis of $100. A owns all of the X stock with a basis of $200. A sells half of the X stock to Y for $200.

Alternatives:

(a)   Would the result necessarily change if X owns only pure preferred stock of Y?

(b)   What if A owns only two of X's 100 outstanding shares and sells one to Y for $4?

(c)   What if A sells 50 shares of X to Z, a newly formed, wholly owned subsidiary of Y?

ADD TO ASSIGNMENT

Cases: Rohinton K. Bhada, 89 TC 959 (1987) (aff'd)

(d)   Instead of $200 in cash, what if A receives from Y pure preferred Y stock with FMV of $200?

(5) A owns all of the X stock with a basis of $200. A buys all of the stock of Y for $50. Later, when the stock of Y is worth $250, A pledges the Y stock as collateral for a $200 loan. A then transfers the Y stock to X in exchange for 10 more shares of X stock worth $50. X assumes the $200 debt.

Alternative: A has just bought all the Y stock in a public tender offer for $50 cash plus $200 in notes.

ADD TO ASSIGNMENT

Code: §§ 1361(b)(2)(A), 1368(a)–1368(c), 1371(a)(2)

(6) A and B each own 50 shares of Y stock with a basis of $100 each. A owns all of the X stock with a basis of $200. X is an S corporation with $100 of old C corporation E&P and $100 AAA. A sells the 50 Y shares to X for $200.

§ 304 CHART

	Seller's income (amount and type)	Seller's basis in remaining stock of each corporation	E&P effect	Acquirer's basis in purchased stock
Bro/sis sale if § 302(a) applies				
Bro/sis sale if §§ 302(d)/301 applies				
Par/sub sale if § 302(a) applies				
Par/sub sale if §§ 302(d)/301 applies				

Distributions of a Corporation's Own Stock and Stock Rights

7A   Nontaxable Stock Distributions; Preferred Stock Bailouts

SUBJECT: Distributions of stock and stock rights that are not taxed to the shareholder upon receipt—Later consequences of nontaxable receipt of preferred stock—Meaning of "bailout" [*Note*: Legislation in 2003, under which dividends are taxed at the same rate as capital gains (with a top rate of 15 percent for both), has greatly reduced the importance of these transactions.]

ASSIGNMENT

B&E: ¶¶ 8.40, 8.41[1], 8.41[4], 8.42[1], 8.42[3]; 12.45; Chapter 8, Part D

Code: Primary: §§ 1(h)(11), 305(a), 305(d), 305(f), 306, 307; Ancillary: §§ 311(a), 312(d), 317(a), 1223(5)

Regs: §§ 1.302-3(a), 1.305-1(a), 1.306-1-1.306-3, 1.307-1, 1.307-2, 1.312-1(e)

Cases: Eisner v. Macomber, 252 US 189 (1920); Chamberlin v. CIR, 207F2d 462 (6th Cir. 1953)

Other materials: Complete the chart at the end of the problems to aid in understanding § 306

PROBLEMS

Note: Assume in all problems that § 305(b) does not apply.

(1) X's common stock (its only class) is traded on the NYSE. X has $1 million E&P. Since X believes its shares are more attractive if they trade below $100, when the shares reach $110, X declares a three-for-one stock split and mails certificates for double the number of shares currently held to all shareholders actually holding certificates. A currently holds a certificate for 100 X shares, bought for $9,000. A receives a new certificate for 200 shares. What are the tax consequences to A and X?

Alternative: X does not care about its share prices and distributes pro rata to its shareholders warrants to buy one common share of X per common share currently owned. The warrant exercise price is $100. The warrant issuance does not affect the $110 trading price of X shares. The warrants also trade on an established market and A quickly sells the warrants received for $1,000.

(2) A and B organized X 15 years ago, each contributing $10,000 and each receiving 100 shares of common stock. Five years ago in June, X declared a one-for-one dividend payable in pure preferred stock (paying a 6 percent cumulative dividend on its par value, which equaled its then $100 of FMV). The value of the common stock after the distribution was $400 per share. In that year, X had accumulated E&P of $13,000 and current E&P of $3,000. In the current year, X has accumulated E&P of $28,000 and current E&P of $2,000. What are the tax consequences of the disposition described in each situation below?

    (a)   In December of the current year, A sells all of A's preferred stock to C for $9,000; In June of the next year, A sells all of A's common stock to D for $50,000.

Alternatives:

      (i)   The sale to *D* took place in June of the current year. Also, what if *C* were *A*'s son?

      (ii)   Same as (i) above except that *A* sells the preferred back to *X*.

ADD TO ASSIGNMENT

Code: §§ 1361(b)(1)(D), 1368(b), 1368(c)

      (iii)   *X* was an S corporation five years ago, with a $20,000 AAA in addition to the $13,000 accumulated E&P but no current E&P.

  (b)   *B*, who is *A*'s son, took over as *X*'s CEO five years ago. *A* gave 100 common shares of *X* to *B* four years ago. *A* dies on December 1 of the current year when the preferred stock is worth $9,000. No election is made under § 2032. In March of the next year, *A*'s executor sells the preferred for $10,000.

ADVANCED ASSIGNMENT

  (c)   In December of the current year, *X* redeems all of *A*'s preferred stock in exchange for $9,000. In the next year, *X* redeems all of *B*'s preferred stock for $9,000; *X*'s available E&P next year is $1,000, before reduction for distributions.

  (d)   In December of the current year, *X* redeems all of *A*'s preferred shares and 50 of *A*'s common shares for a total consideration of $34,000, of which $9,000 is properly allocable to the preferred and $25,000 to the common.

      Alternative: X had neither accumulated nor current E&P five years ago.

§ 306 CHART

	Sale of § 306 Stock	Redemption of § 306 Stock
When is relevant E&P measured?		
Is the transaction treated as a true dividend?		
What is the amount of E&P taint?		

7B   Taxable Stock Distributions

SUBJECT: Discerning real stock distributions that will generate gross income to the recipient—Discerning other events that will generate deemed stock distributions that can be taxable [*Note*: As a result of 2003 legislation, taxability here will be at the same rate as capital gains (generally 15 percent).]

ASSIGNMENT

B&E: ¶¶ 8.40–8.41

Code: §§ 1(h)(11), 305(b)

Regs: §§ 1.305-1(b)(1), 1.305-3(a), 1.305-3(e), Ex. (2), 1.312-1(d)

Cases: Koshland v. Helvering, 298 US 441 (1936)

PROBLEMS

Assumptions: X has ample E&P, *X* regularly pays annual cash dividends on all stock, and *X* pays interest on any outstanding debt each year. In problems involving two classes of stock outstanding, the two classes are not held in the same proportions by the shareholders. Determine for each problem the tax results to all affected shareholders and to *X*.

(1)   *X* has three classes of stock, Class A common, Class B common, and nonconvertible preferred. Each of the common classes has 30 shares outstanding, worth $10 per share. What will be the tax treatment of the shareholders as a result of the following transactions?

     (a)   *X* distributes one share of common (FMV $10) on each 10 shares of common outstanding.

ADD TO ASSIGNMENT

Regs: § 1.305-2(b), Ex. (1)

     (b)   Change (1)(a), above, to give the common shareholders the option to receive cash of $10 per share in lieu of the stock. Would the answer change if the cash option were for $9.90?

ADD TO ASSIGNMENT

Regs: § 1.305-5(a)

     (c)   *X* distributes one share of common (or of preferred) on each share of preferred.

ADD TO ASSIGNMENT

Regs: § 1.305-4

     (d)   *X* distributes common on Class A and preferred on Class B.

ADD TO ASSIGNMENT

Regs: § 1.305-3(e), Ex. (1)

(e) X distributes common on the Class A common and distributes cash on the Class B common. Also, what if X is an S corporation? (See Code §§ 1368(a)–1368(c).)

ADD TO ASSIGNMENT

Code: § 1036

Regs: §§ 1.305-3(b), 1.305-3(e), Ex. (3)

(f) X distributes one share of the same class of preferred as the preferred outstanding on each 10 shares of common.

ADD TO ASSIGNMENT

Regs: § 1.305-6

(g) Change (1)(f), above, to assume that the distribution is a new class of convertible junior preferred. Conversion must be elected within four months of issue. The conversion ratio is based on equal market values as of the date of distribution of the junior preferred.

ADD TO ASSIGNMENT

Code: §§ 305(c), 1059(e)(1)

Regs: §§ 1.305-7(a), 1.305-7(c), 1.305-3(b)(3), 1.305-3(e), Exs. (8)– (13), 1.305-5(d), Exs. (2), (6)

Other materials: Rev. Rul. 86-25, 1986-1 CB 202

(2) Using the basic facts of problem (1):

(a)   What would result if X redeems for $10 cash per share one third of the B common on a pro rata basis. Since we are not told the voting power of the classes, determine the results assuming that the redemption is treated as a cash distribution and assuming that it is treated as an exchange. In addition, determine the results assuming that the redemption is an isolated event. Alternatively, assume that the redemption is part of a continuing series of redemptions.

(b)   Alternately, X adopts a plan of reorganization (actually a "recapitalization") and exchanges a new class of common for all of Class A common and a new class of preferred for all of Class B common.

ADD TO ASSIGNMENT

Regs: § 1.305-5(b)

(3) X issues to C, for $100 per share, X preferred stock that the owner can put back to X for $150 per share in five years.

(a)   In addition: X can, but is not required to, call the stock for redemption at $150 at any time.

Alternative:

(b)   The shareholder has no put although X can, but is not required to, call the stock at $150 after five years.

ADD TO ASSIGNMENT

Regs: §§ 1.305-3(d) (scan), 1.305-3(e), Exs. (4)–(7), 1.305-7(b)

(4) X has only common stock outstanding. X also has convertible debt outstanding. Upon conversion, the debt holder gets 10 shares of X common

per $100 face amount of debt. *X* distributes one share of common on each 10 shares of common outstanding. What would result and how could § 305(b) be avoided?

7C   Recapitalizations (Part One)

SUBJECT: Reorganizations that change the capital structure of a single corporation by its exchanges of new stock for outstanding stock [*Note:* Debt for debt, stock for debt, debt for stock, and combinations are covered in Lesson 15: Recapitalizations (Part Two); nonqualified preferred and other "boot" issues are covered here as well as in Lesson 9. Note that recapitalizations routinely also involve §§ 305 and 306.]

ASSIGNMENT

B&E: Primary: ¶¶ 12.27[1], 12.27[2]; Secondary: ¶¶ 8.62[2], 12.44[3], 12.45

Code: §§ 305(c), 306(a)(1)(D), 306(c)(1)(B), 306(c)(1)(C), 351(g), 354(a)(1), 358(a), 358(b)(1), 368(a)(1)(E), 1032, 1036

Regs: §§ 1.305-5(d), Ex. (6), 1.305-7(c), 1.306-3(d), 1.368-2(e), 1.1002-1(c), 1.1036-1

PROBLEMS

Assumptions: Each of the exchanges effected in these problems is pursuant to a "plan" of reorganization and has a good business purpose. Each transaction qualifies as a Type E reorganization under § 368(a)(1)(E).

In each problem (except as otherwise stated) determine the tax consequences of the described exchanges to the affected shareholders and to *X*.

New Stock for Old Stock-Equity Swaps

(1)   *A* is one of the minority shareholders of closely held *X*, which has only one class of stock outstanding and plenty of E&P. *X* hopes to make a public offering of common at some time in the future and, in preparation, causes all its shareholders to exchange their common shares pro rata for a new class of

48

common (different from the class that may be sold to the public) plus preferred shares. *A* swaps stock with a basis of $100 for new common worth $400 and preferred worth $100. Also if *A* later sells the preferred for $110, what are *A*'s tax consequences?

(2)   *A* is the founding, majority shareholder and CEO of *X. A* will retire and exchange all common stock owned (basis $100,000, FMV $1 million) for all of a new class of nonvoting preferred with a stated par value of $1 million and paying a 10 percent annual cumulative dividend. The rest of *X*'s common stock is owned by *A*'s son, the new CEO. Under §§ 2701 through 2704, the value of the preferred is $1 million for transfer tax purposes, so there is no deemed transfer of value to the son.

   (a)   Alternatively, the rest of the stock is owned by unrelated persons and the preferred pays a 2 percent cumulative dividend, is worth $1 million, and is mandatorily callable at *A*'s death for $2 million. [Hint: *A*'s life expectancy is 10 years; Rev. Rul. 83-119 deemed the life expectancy to be the redemption date.]

   (b)   Alternatively to (a) above, *A* swapped his common for preferred without a redemption feature (but paying a preferred dividend) and shares of a new class of nonvoting common, while the remaining shareholders swapped their old common for a new class of voting common plus some of the nonvoting common.

   (c)   What results in this problem (2) if the preferred is § 351(g) nonqualified preferred stock?

Note: For other recap variations, see Lesson 15.

Complete Liquidations

8A   General

SUBJECT: Taxable acquisitions and consequences of corporate liquidation, to a corporation and its shareholders, where § 332 does not apply to S corporation liquidation and § 1374

ASSIGNMENT

B&E: ¶¶ 10.01, 10.02, 10.03, 10.06, 10.07, 10.08

Code: §§ 331, 346(a), 1001, 1012, 1231(a)(1)–1231(a)(3), 1231(b)(1)

Regs: §§ 1.331-1, 1.332-2(c) (for definition of "liquidation")

PROBLEMS

Assumptions for problems (1) through (7): X owns a rental building (its only asset) with a gross FMV of $1,000, subject to a nonrecourse mortgage of $400. X's adjusted basis for this building is $300. A owns all of X's stock, with a total basis of $100. X has $200 of E&P. X is on the accrual method of accounting and reports on the calendar year. Assume that the corporate tax payable by X on $700 gain is $250 and on $600 gain is $200.

     For each of the following problems (1) through (7) below, determine the amounts and character of realized and recognized gain or loss to all parties, the time of recognition, and the transferee's basis in any property received in kind.

(1)   X sells the building, subject to the mortgage, to B in the current year for $600 in cash. X then liquidates, distributing to A all of the cash remaining after paying its taxes, in cancellation of A's stock in the current year.

Alternatives:

(a)   *B* pays $300 cash and gives *B*'s $300 note payable in equal annual installments over five years. *X*'s plan of liquidation provides that *X* will stay in existence for five years for the sole purpose of collecting the note and paying the net amount over to *A* annually.

ADD TO ASSIGNMENT

Code: §§ 453(a), 453(h), 453B(a)

Regs: § 15A.453-1 (through 15A.453-1(b)(3)(i))

(b)   *B* pays $300 in cash and gives *B*'s $300 (face and FMV) note payable in equal annual installments plus interest over 5 years. In liquidation, *X* distributes the net cash and the note to *A* in the year of sale.

ADD TO ASSIGNMENT

B&E: ¶ 6.09[5]

Code: §§ 165(f), 453(a), 453B(h), 1211(b), 1212(b)(1), 1363(a)

(c)   Change the facts in (1) and (1)(b) above to assume that *X* is an S corporation and § 1374 does not apply.

ADD TO ASSIGNMENT

B&E: ¶¶ 10.04, 10.05

Code: §§ 334(a), 336(a), 336(b), 1211(b), 1239(a), 6901(a)(1)(A)(i), 7701(g)

Regs: §§ 1.334-1(a), 1.1001-2(a)

Cases: Arrowsmith v. CIR, 344 US 6 (1952)

(2)   *X* adopts a plan of complete liquidation and distributes the property to *A* "in kind" pursuant to this plan. *A* then sells the property to *B* for $600 in cash, with *B* taking subject to the $400 mortgage. Would it matter if *A*'s shares had varying prices per share? What if the property were subject to contingent environmental liabilities?

Alternative: X is an S corporation and § 1374 does not apply.

ADD TO ASSIGNMENT

Code: §§ 1366(f)(2), 1374(a), 1374(b)(1), 1374(c), 1374(d)(1), 1374(d)(3)

(3)   *A* sells the stock in *X* to *B* for $600 in cash. *B* promptly liquidates *X* to get direct ownership of, and a $1,000 basis in, the building. Was *B* wise to pay $600? Could *B* obtain a better tax result by electing S corporation status for *X* before liquidating *X*?

Alternative: X always had been an S corporation.

ADD TO ASSIGNMENT

Code: § 1016(a)(1)

Regs: § 15A.453-1(d)(2)(iii)

(4)   Suppose that in (1) above, the gross FMV of *X*'s property is actually $1,000, but to induce *X* to sell, *B* also gives *X* a "contingent" right (with no ascertainable FMV) to receive from *B* an additional $500 in 5 years if *B* earns profits from the building in excess of any profits it historically had earned.

ADD TO ASSIGNMENT

Code: §§ 172(b)(1)(A), 267(a)(1), 267(b)(2), 336(d)(1), 1244(a)

(5)   Suppose that in (2) above, the basis for X's property is $1,500 instead of $300? Would your answer change if A had organized X two years ago by contributing the building then worth $1,500 with a $1,500 basis in exchange for all the stock and A's stock basis is now $1,500 (assume no debt is involved)?

ADD TO ASSIGNMENT

Code: §§ 1060, 7701(g)

Regs: §§ 1.1001-2(a)(3), 1.338-6T(c)(4)

(6)   Suppose that in (2) above, the value of X's property is $350 and X liquidates with A taking subject to the $400 mortgage. A then sells to B subject to the mortgage and for no additional consideration.

ADD TO ASSIGNMENT

Code: §§ 1014, 1375

Regs: § 1.1374-4(h)(1)

(7) X has one shareholder, A, whose stock basis is $100. X operates a business in a building whose value is $1,000, with an adjusted basis of $300. X has $1,000 in the bank. In the current year, X sells its operating business assets for $1,000 cash, which increases X's total E&P to $1,500. Also in the current year, in exchange for other assets X receives an installment note reportable under § 453, enters into a lease for the building with the buyers of its business, and retains part of its inventory for gradual sale in the future. A, who is age 70, comes to you after all these steps have been taken and inquires whether X

should be liquidated or should elect S corporation status to avoid paying double tax on the installment gain, the rent, the future inventory sales, and a possible sale of the building in a few years. What do you advise?

8B   Subsidiary Liquidations and § 338

SUBJECT: Taxable acquisitions and liquidations of corporations controlled by an 80 percent corporate shareholder—How an acquiring corporation can get FMV basis in the assets of an acquired corporation despite the normal carryover basis regime and the costs of that choice

ASSIGNMENT

B&E: ¶¶ 10.20–10.22, 14.20–14.21[2]

Code: §§ 332, 334(b), 337, 381(a)(1), 1504(a)(2), 1504(a)(4)

Regs: §§ 1.332-1–1.332-4, 1.334-1(b)

PROBLEMS

Assumptions: Y owns 100 percent of the stock of X (all common) with a basis of $100. X owns a rental building (its only asset) with a gross FMV of $ 1,000, subject to a nonrecourse mortgage of $400. X's adjusted basis in this building is $300. X has $200 of E&P. X is on the accrual method of accounting and reports on the calendar year. X and Y do not report on a consolidated basis.

For each of the following problems, determine the character and amounts of realized and recognized gain or loss to all parties, the time of recognition, the transferee's basis in any property received in kind, and any E&P impact.

(1)   X sells its building to Z for $600 cash, subject to the debt, pays its tax, and liquidates.

(2) *X* distributes the building to *Y* in complete liquidation and *Y* sells the building to *Z* for $600 cash, subject to the debt.

ADD TO ASSIGNMENT

B&E: ¶ 10.42

Code: §§ 269(b), 338

Regs: §§ 1.338-3(d) (2001), 1.338(h)(10)-1T (2003)

Cases: Kimbell-Diamond Milling Co. v. CIR, 14 TC 74, aff'd per curiam, 187 F2d 718 (5th Cir.), cert. denied, 342 US 827 (1951)

Other materials: Rev. Rul. 90-95, 1990-2 CB 67; Rev. Rul. 2001-46, 2001-42 IRB 321

(3) *Y* sells the *X* stock to *Z* for $600 and *Z* liquidates *X*. Should *Z* make a § 338 election instead of liquidating *X*? In answering this question, describe how § 338 would work on these facts. Can you think of other facts that would make a § 338 election attractive? What if *X*'s basis in the building is $1,500, § 338 is not elected, and *Z* liquidates *X* within two years? Was *Z* wise in agreeing to this deal under the original facts? If you represented *Z* and were intent on negotiating the built-in tax out of the stock price, and if *Y* and *X* file a consolidated return, what would you recommend?

Alternative: X's basis in the building is $500.

(4) Same as (2) above, except *X*'s debt is $1,100, not $400.

ADD TO ASSIGNMENT

B&E: ¶ 10.23

Code: § 1271(a)(1)

Regs: § 1.332-7

(5)   Same as (2) above, except the $400 debt is owed to *Y* in the form of a $400 bond of *X* (that *Y* purchased for $300 in the market).

(6)   Same as (2) above, except *Y* owes money to *X*.

ADD TO ASSIGNMENT

B&E: ¶ 14.45

Code: § 384

Note: The following questions preview matters covered later in the course.

(7)   Same as (3) above, except *Z* has large NOLs.

ADD TO ASSIGNMENT

B&E: ¶ 10.24

Regs: § 1.332-5

(8)   Same as (2) above, except there is also outstanding a class of *X*'s pure preferred stock, which represents half of *X*'s equity value and which is entitled to half of *X*'s net asset value upon liquidation, but of which *Y* owns none. [Don't do the numbers; just state what happens.]

ADD TO ASSIGNMENT

B&E: ¶¶ 12.63[2], 14.40

(9)   Same as (8) above, except that instead of liquidating, *X* merges into *Y*.

Alternative: *Y* merges into *X*.

8C Penalty Taxes and Collapsible Corporations

SUBJECT: The accumulated earnings tax—The personal holding company tax—Conversion of capital gains into ordinary income in connection with collapsible corporations

ASSIGNMENT

B&E: Chapter 7; Chapter 10, Part D

Code: §§ 341–346, 531–537, 541–547

Cases: Pat O'Brien, 25 TC 376 (1955); Rutter Rex Mfg. Co. v. CIR, 853 F2d 1275 (5th Cir. 1988); Technalysis Corp., 101 TC No. 27 (1993); Pleasant Summit Land Corp. v. CIR, 863, F2d 263 (3d Cir. 1988)

Note: There are no problems accompanying this lesson.

Legislation enacted in 2003 materially softened the pain of §§ 531 and 541 by reducing the tax rate to 15 percent; even better, this same legislation finally repealed § 341 as "deadwood" (although very dense deadwood to be sure as many former students became totally lost in its thickets).

Introduction to Corporate Reorganizations

Introduction: Reorganizations are one of the few remaining ways to exchange property without current recognition of gain (or loss). Most reorganization issues relate either to (1) characterizing the transaction as a reorganization or (2) determining the tax consequences to the parties of such characterization. Because the second set of issues is common to all types of reorganizations, we will overview that set first, assuming a proper characterization of the transaction as a reorganization.

The tax categories of reorganizations (using the term broadly) can be grouped in various ways. Under the approach of this Lesson, Lessons 10 through 15, and Lesson 17, reorganizations come in four basic types:

1. Reorganizations involving one corporation (Type E (also known as recapitalizations): § 368(a)(1)(E); Type F: § 368(a)(1)(F));

2. Reorganizations involving acquisition of assets of a target corporation by another corporation (Type A: § 368(a)(1)(A); Type C: § 368(a)(1)(C); nondivisive Type D: § 368(a)(1)(D)); Type G: § 368(a)(1)(G);

3. Reorganizations involving acquisition of stock of a target corporation by another corporation (Type B: § 368(a)(1)(B));

4. Triangular variants on the Type A, B, and C reorganization (§§ 368(a)(2)(C), 368(a)(2)(D), 368(a)(2)(E)); and

5. Reorganizations involving division of a single corporation (divisive reorganizations: § 368(a)(1)(D) and/or § 355).

In every reorganization, one or more (but not necessarily all) of the following potentially taxable § 1001 dispositions of property will occur:

Disposition 1:   Exchange by the target corporation of its assets principally for stock of another corporation.

Disposition 2:   Distribution of such stock and possibly other property by the target to its shareholders and possibly to its creditors.

Disposition 3:   Exchange with the target by its shareholders and creditors of their stock or debt for the distributed stock and any other property.

Dispositions 2 and 3 are obviously opposite ends of the same exchange.

SUBJECT: Because the paradigm reorganization types from the viewpoint of illustrating the tax results of all three of these dispositions are the Type A and C reorganizations, and Type C sets these out most boldly, this is a brief introduction to the function of reorganizations and a study of Dispositions 1, 2, and 3, principally in the context of the Type C reorganization.

ASSIGNMENT

B&E: ¶¶ 12.01–12.05

Code: §§ 368(a)(1)(B), 368(a)(1)(C), 453(f)(4), 453(f)(5), 1031(a)(2)(B)

Regs: §§ 1.1001-1(a), 1.1002-1(c)

PROBLEMS

Assumptions: A owns all of the stock of *T*, the only asset of which is acreage that had been used as one of the last surviving drive-in theatres, with an adjusted basis of $60,000 and a fair market value of $150,000. *A*'s basis in the *T* stock is $50,000. *Y*, a publicly held grocery chain, wants to acquire the property for a store site. *Y* is willing to give either its voting common stock worth $150,000 in exchange for the property in a taxable transaction or its stock worth $130,000 in exchange for the property or for the stock of *T* in a transaction that will be tax-free to *A* and *T*.

(1)   Can *A* avoid gain recognition by a like kind exchange of *T* stock for *Y* stock under § 1031? Under any other section? If *Y* offers to exchange one of its publicly traded bonds for the *T* stock, should *A* accept the offer? Why is *Y* willing to give only $130,000 worth of stock in a tax-free exchange?

ADD TO ASSIGNMENT

B&E: ¶¶ 12.21, 12.24, 12.40, 12.42, 12.43, 12.44, 12.61[2]

Code: §§ 336(c), 354, 356, 358, 361, 362(b), 368(a)(1)(A), 368(a)(1)(C), 368(b), 381(a)(2), 1032

(2)   The parties agree on a Type C reorganization, with *T* trading the land for *Y* stock worth $130,000 and then liquidating. *Y* will give *T* some treasury shares *Y* bought in the market for $100,000. Assume this will qualify as a good Type C reorganization to which *T* and *Y* are "parties to a reorganization" (i.e., *T* and *Y* are on the § 368(b) "guest list").

(a)   Upon Disposition 1, how much gain will *T* realize and recognize?

Alternative: What if *T* had received $1,000 cash in addition to the *Y* stock?

(b)   Upon Disposition 2, how much gain will *T* recognize?

(c)   Upon Disposition 3, how much gain will *A* realize and recognize? What will be *A*'s basis in the *Y* stock?

Alternative: What if *A* had received $1,000 cash in lieu of $1,000 worth of the *Y* stock?

(d)   How much gain will *Y* recognize upon exchanging its treasury shares for the land?

(e)   What will be Y's basis in the land? Would Y's basis increase if Y also gave $1,000 cash to T?

(f)   What happens to the tax history of T, such as liability for tax deficiencies for past years, NOLs, and E&P?

(3)   Can you suggest another type of reorganization involving an asset acquisition by Y without recognition of income by A?

(4)   If Y were willing to take A's stock in T in a Type B reorganization, describe the results in Dispositions 1, 2, and 3, if any, and determine Y's basis in the shares acquired. What happens to T's E&P?

ADD TO ASSIGNMENT

Cases: Helvering v. Gregory, 69 F2d 809 (2d Cir. 1934); Gregory v. Helvering, 293 US 465 (1935); West Coast Marketing Corp. v. CIR, 46 TC 32 (1966)

(5)   Would your answer to (4) above change if A had just incorporated T by contributing the property for T's stock?

ADD TO ASSIGNMENT

Code: § 1036

(6)   Alternately, B owns some nonvoting common stock of T (a class of common different from that owned by A), and B swaps some of that stock for some of A's voting common stock.

Reorganizations Involving Stock Acquisitions: Type B

SUBJECT: Nontriangular Type B reorganizations—Like Type C, a "solely for voting stock" reorganization—"No boot in a B"—Golden parachutes

Note: This lesson may be assigned after Lesson 11. If Lesson 9 is not assigned before this lesson, read the introduction to that lesson.

ASSIGNMENT

B&E: ¶¶ 5.04[7], 12.01–12.21, 12.23 (key), 12.43[3], 12.44[1], 12.44[3], 12.61[2]

Code: §§ 306(c)(1)(B), 338(h)(3), 351(a), 354, 358(e), 362(b), 368(a)(1)(B), 368(b), 368(c), 1001(c), 1032

Regs: §§ 1.368-2(c), 1.368-2(j)(7), Exs. (4), (5); §§ 1.368-1(e)(1)(ii), 1.368-1(e)(6), Ex. (9) (Aug. 31, 2000)

Cases: Reeves, 71 TC 727 (1979), vacated and remanded sub. nom Chapman v. CIR, 618 F2d 856 (1st Cir. 1980) (for the Service's position, see Rev. Rul. 75-123, 1975-1 CB 115)

Other materials: Rev. Rul. 67-274, 1967-2 CB 141; Rev. Rul. 67-448, 1967-2 CB 144 (the "forced B"); Rev. Rul. 72-354, 1972-2 CB 216; Rev. Rul. 73-54, 1973-1 CB 187; Rev. Rul. 98-10, 1998-1 CB 643

PROBLEMS

Assumptions: T has 100 shares of voting common stock outstanding, which are owned 50 shares by *A* (basis $200), 30 shares by *B* (basis $400), and 20 shares by *C* (basis $150). *T* owns the following assets:

	Basis	Value
Nonoperating assets	$200	$300
Operating assets	$700	$900
Totals	$900	$1,200

T owes $200 (in the form of 20-year bonds held by L with an adjusted basis of $190) and has E&P of $200. Assume that each T share is worth $10 and that property exchanged therefor is worth $10. Unless otherwise indicated, (1) each transaction has a proper business purpose, (2) there is a continuity of T's "business enterprise," (3) the transaction is pursuant to a "plan of reorganization," and (4) the face amount of debt is its FMV. P is a publicly held corporation whose stock is traded on the NYSE.

What are the tax consequences to A, B, C, L, T, and P from the following transactions?

(1) On January 2 of the current year, P acquires all of the T common stock from A, B, and C, as a result of separate negotiations with each shareholder, solely in exchange for voting preferred stock of P.

Alternative:

(a) T is a public company. P acquires 100 percent of T's stock by a public tender offer and immediately liquidates T.

(b) *In addition:* P also purchases the T bonds from L for $200 cash.

Alternative: P swaps its own 15-year registered bonds for the T bonds held by L.

(c) *In addition:* P also agrees to advance $100 in cash to T.

Alternative:

(d) T is an S corporation and the stock basis of A, B, and C is $500, $300, and $200, respectively, reflecting in part $300 passed-through but undistributed income of T as an S corporation.

(2)   On January 2 of the current year, *P* acquires all of the *T* common stock from *A*, *B*, and *C* for $200 in cash and *P* voting stock with FMV of $800, the consideration being allocated ratably among *A*, *B*, and *C* in proportion to their *T* stockholdings.

Alternative: The exchange was conducted as a "share exchange" pursuant to an agreement of reorganization between *T* and *P*. *C* dissented and *P* supplied the cash to buy *C*'s shares.

(3)   On January 2 of the current year, *P* acquires all of *C*'s *T* stock for cash. On July 1 of the current year, *P* acquires all of *B*'s *T* stock solely for *P* voting stock. On December 1 of the current year, *P* acquires all of *A*'s *T* stock solely for *P* voting stock. [*Note:* In reality, these three transactions occurring within 11 months would be difficult to separate under Regs. § 1.368.2(c).] What if, alternatively:

   (a)   Each transaction is a separate "acquisition."

   (b)   Each transaction is part of a single overall "acquisition."

   (c)   The first transaction is a separate "acquisition," but the last two are part of a single overall "acquisition."

   (d)   The first two transactions are part of a single overall "acquisition," but the last is a separate acquisition.

(4)   On January 2 of the current year, *T* redeems *B*'s and *C*'s *T* stock for cash and notes. *P* then acquires all of *A*'s *T* stock solely in exchange for *P* voting stock worth $500.

Alternative: *A*'s and *C*'s *T* stock is redeemed by *T* for cash and notes. *P* then acquires *B*'s *T* stock solely in exchange for *P* voting stock worth $300.

(5)   On January 2 of the current year, *P* acquires all of the *T* common stock from *A*, *B*, and *C* solely in exchange for voting preferred stock of *P*. What would result in each of the following alternative situations?

(a)   *T* first declares a dividend of its nonoperating assets and distributes all of those assets to *A*, *B*, and *C* pro rata. (In this situation, *A*, *B*, and *C* are corporations.)

(b)   *P* agrees to pay the costs of registering its common stock when *A*, *B*, and *C* wish to sell it.

(c)   *P* agrees to pay any transfer taxes arising from the exchange.

(d)   *P* agrees to pay all legal and accounting fees attributable to the exchange.

(e)   *A* and *B* are also the principal employees of *T*. *A* and *B* entered into employment agreements with *T* (with *P*'s acquiescence) just before the stock swap, which guaranteed them employment with *T* for two years at twice their current salaries (noncancelable) by *T* except for gross misconduct) and allowed them to quit at any time during the two years and be paid for the remainder of that period. *C* opposed the entry of the contracts by *T*. *T*'s nonoperating assets include 100 percent of the outstanding stock of *X*.

(6)   *P* exchanges its voting stock with *T* for what constitutes 80 percent of *T*'s outstanding common stock, its only class outstanding.

(7)   Ignoring the basic assumptions of these problems, *T* is 80 percent owned by *P* and merges into *P*. *P* receives 100 percent of the outstanding stock of *X* (*T*'s only asset); *T*'s minority shareholders receive *P* voting stock.

Alternative: Instead of a merger, *T* swaps its (appreciated) *X* stock with *P* for *P* voting stock.

Reorganizations Involving Asset Acquisitions

11A   Type A Reorganizations

SUBJECT: Nontriangular Type A reorganizations—The continuity-of-proprietary-interest requirement

Note: If Lesson 9 is not assigned before this lesson, read the introduction to that lesson.

ASSIGNMENT

B&E: ¶¶ 6.05, 6.09, 12.02–12.21, 12.22 (key), 12.40–12.44, 12.61, 12.66, 12.67, 14.21[3], 14.23[2]

Code: §§ 302, 312(a), 312(b), 312(d)(1), 312(n)(7), 318, 368(a)(1)(A), 368(b), 354–362 (as they relate to Type A reorganizations), 381, 1012, 1032, 1362(d)(2), 1362(g), 1371(a), 1371(e), 1374, 1377(b)

Regs: §§ 1.354-1(e), 1.356-3(b), 1.368-1(d), 1.368-1(e), 1.368-2(a), 1.368-2(b)(1), 1.368-2T(b)(1) (2003), 1.368-2(f), 1.368-2(g), 1.368-2(h), 1.381(c)(2)-1(c)(1), 1.1001-3(e)(4)(i)

Cases: Cortland Specialty Co. v. CIR, 60 F2d 937 (2d Cir. 1932), cert. denied, 288 US 599 (1933); Pinellas Ice & Cold Storage Co. v. CIR, 287 US 462 (1933); John A. Nelson Co. v. Helvering, 296 US 374 (1935); LeTulle v. Scofield, 308 US 415 (1940); Helvering v. Alabama Asphaltic Limestone Co., 315 US 179 (1942); Helvering v. Minnesota Tea Co., 296 US 378 (1935); May B. Kass, 60 TC 218 (1973); Penrod, 88 TC 1415 (1987); McDonald's Restaurants of Ill., Inc. v. CIR, 688 F2d 520 (7th Cir.

1982); CIR v. Clark, 489 US 726 (1989); J. E. Seagram Corp., 104 TC 75 (1995); Archie Honbarrier, 115 TC 300 (2000)

Other materials: Rev. Rul. 78-250, 1978-2 CB 83; Rev. Proc. 77-37, 1977-2 CB 42; Rev. Proc. 86-42, 1986-2 CB 722; Rev. Proc. 90-56, 1990-2 CB 639; Rev. Rul. 93-61, 1993-2 CB 118; Rev. Rul. 99-58, 1999-52 IRB 701; Rev. Rul. 2000-5, 2000-5 IRB 436; Rev. Rul. 2001-46, 2001-42 IRB 321

PROBLEMS

Assumptions: T is a closely held corporation with 100 shares of voting common stock outstanding, which are owned 50 shares by A (adjusted basis $200), 30 shares by B (adjusted basis $400), and 20 shares by C (adjusted basis $150). T owns the following assets:

	Basis	*Value*
Nonoperating assets	$200	$300
Operating assets	$700	$900
Totals	$900	$1,200

T owes outstanding liabilities of $200 (in the form of a 20-year bond held by L at an adjusted basis of $200), and T has E&P of $400. Assume each T share is worth $10. P is a publicly held corporation whose stock is listed on the New York Stock Exchange. Unless otherwise indicated, (1) each transaction has a proper business purpose; (2) there is continuity of T 's "business enterprise" in P, (3) the transaction is pursuant to a "plan of reorganization," and (4) FMV of debt is also its face amount and adjusted issue price. In each problem below, L consented to and did receive a bond of P that is identical in terms to the bond of T that L exchanged therefor.

What are the tax consequences to T, P, A, B, C, and L from the following transactions?

(1)   T merges into P under state law. T 's shareholders receive pro rata $1,000 FMV of P's nonvoting, nonparticipating, nonconvertible 8 percent cumulative ("pure" or "straight") preferred stock.

Alternative 1: T's debt to L is either $1,000 or $1,300 (and the consideration given by P is appropriately adjusted).

Alternative 2: *T* and/or *P* are foreign corporations and the merger occurs under the laws of England.

(2)   Same as (1) above, but instead of preferred stock, *T*'s shareholders receive pro rata $200 FMV of *P*'s two-year notes, $400 FMV of *P*'s 20-year registered bonds, and $400 FMV of *P*'s voting common stock.

Alternative: Before the merger, *P*'s voting common stock is 100 percent owned by E, A's father; after the merger, E owns 70 percent of *P*'s voting common stock.

(3)   *T* merges into *P* solely in exchange for *P* voting stock (and the debt assumption). *B*, however, dissents under state law procedure for objecting shareholders. *B*'s *T* stock is purchased by *T* under an agreement whereby *B* agrees to take the $300 nonoperating assets, and whereby the stock given by *P* is reduced to $700. [State the results generally, but do the numbers for *B* only.]

(4)   Same as (3) above, *A* also dissents and likewise is bought out for $500 worth of the operating assets. *P* gives *T* only $200 in value of *P* stock. Will *P* be concerned about this result (aside from the loss of *T*'s assets)? What would you advise *P* to do to protect itself?

(5)   *T* merges into *P* solely in exchange for *P* voting stock. Within six months of the merger, *A*, *B*, and *C* sell all of their *P* stock in a disposition they had planned at the time of the merger. What if, at the time of the merger, *A*, *B*, and *C* planned to keep the *P* stock.

(6)   *S*, a subsidiary of *P*, merges into *T*, exchanging solely cash for *T*'s outstanding stock. New *T* stock is issued to *P* for its S stock.

In problems (7) and (8) below, assume that *T* is an S corporation. State the general results without doing the numbers.

(7)   Same as the basic facts of (1) above. *T* has $200 AAA.

Alternative: The *T* shareholders receive both *P* debt and *P* voting common stock and before the merger, *P*'s voting common stock is 100-percent-owned by E, *A*'s father. After the merger, E owns 70 percent of *P*'s voting common stock.

(8)   Z, another corporation (but not an S corporation), which is owned by E, F, and G and has E&P, appreciated assets, and common and preferred stock outstanding, is merged into *T* (which had no E&P) solely for *T* nonvoting common stock.

11B   Type C Reorganizations

SUBJECT: Nontriangular Type C reorganizations—The "practical merger"

ASSIGNMENT

B&E: ¶¶ 4.60[1], 12.24 (key), 12.62[1], 12.62[2], 12.65, 12.67[2] (and others assigned in Lesson 11A)

Code: §§ 306(c)(1), 312(h)(2), 331, 334, 336, 368(a)(1)(C), 368(a)(2)(A), 368(a)(2)(B), 368(a)(2)(G), 1016(a)(1), 1060 (and others assigned in Lesson 11A)

Regs: §§ 1.354-1(d), Ex. (4), 1.354-1(e), 1.356-3(b), 1.358-2(a)(2), 1.368-1(d), 1.368-1(e), 1.368-2(d), 1.368-2(f)

Cases: Helvering v. Southwest Consolidated Corp., 315 US 194 (1942)

Other materials: Rev. Rul. 67-274, 1967-2 CB 141; Rev. Rul. 70-271, 1970-1 CB 166 (beware subsequent changes in § 361); Rev. Rul. 2001-46, 2001-42 IRB 321; Rev. Rul. 2003-79, 2003-29 IRB 80; Rev. Proc. 77-37, 1977-2 CB 42; Rev. Proc. 86-42, 1986-2 CB 722

PROBLEMS

Assumptions: *T*'s 100 shares of voting common stock outstanding are owned 50 shares by *A* (adjusted basis $200), 30 shares by *B* (adjusted basis $400), and 20 shares by *C* (adjusted basis $150). *T* owns the following assets:

	Basis	Value
Nonoperating assets	$200	$300
Operating assets	$700	$900
Totals	$900	$1,200

T owes $200 (in the form of a 20-year bond held by *L* at an adjusted basis of $200), and has E&P of $400 before each of the transactions described below. Assume each *T* share is worth $10 and that property exchanged therefor is worth $10. *P* is a publicly held corporation. Unless otherwise indicated, (1) each transaction has a proper business purpose, (2) there is continuity of *T*'s "business enterprise" in *P*, (3) the transaction is pursuant to a "plan of reorganization," and (4) FMV of debt is also its face amount and adjusted issue price. If *T* incurs any tax liability, identify that fact but do not compute the amount (disregard it as a liability of *T*) and do not reduce the stock value of *A*, *B*, and *C* thereby.

In each of the problems below, what are the tax consequences to *T*, *P*, *A*, *B*, *C*, and *L*?

(1) Because *P* is unwilling to assume *T*'s debts, a merger is not feasible, so *T* transfers all its assets to *P* in exchange for the following alternative types of consideration, after which *T* promptly liquidates. Unless otherwise stated, *A*, *B*, and *C* assume the debt to *L* pro rata.

(a) $1,200 FMV of *P*'s notes, payable over five years.

(b) $1,200 FMV of *P*'s bonds, payable in 20 years and convertible into *P* voting common stock during the first five years.

Alternative: $1,200 FMV warrants for acquisition of *P* voting stock.

(c) $1,200 FMV of *P*'s nonvoting 8 percent cumulative preferred stock.

(d)   Same as (c) above, except that the stock is entitled to one vote per share, but the stock in the aggregate constitutes approximately one percent of the *P* outstanding stock vote.

Alternatives: *T*'s debt to *L* is satisfied by:

1.   *T*'s transfer of $200 FMV of *P* stock to *L*;

2.   *T*'s sale of enough stock to pay *L*; or

3.   *P*'s assumption of the debt and reduction of the FMV stock to $1,000.

(2)   *T* transfers all of its operating assets to *P* in exchange for the following alternative types of consideration, after which *T* promptly liquidates:

(a) $900 FMV of *P* voting stock. *T* then sells $200 worth of nonoperating assets to pay *L*.

(b)   Same as (a) above, except *P* also assumes the $200 liability to *L* without issuing a new bond, and *T* receives $700 FMV of *P* stock.

(c)   Same as (a) above, except *T* also retains $100 of its operating assets and receives $800 FMV of *P* stock.

(3)   *T* transfers all of its assets to *P* in exchange for the following alternative types of consideration:

(a) $200 FMV of *P*'s nonvoting preferred stock and $1,000 FMV of *P*'s voting common stock.

(b) $40 FMV of *P*'s two-year notes, assumption of *T*'s $200 bond (without issuance of a new bond), and *P* voting common stock with FMV of $960. In addition, *P* agrees to pay cash to *T* in the amount

72

owing to any dissenting shareholders and for fractional shares, with a proportional reduction in the *P* stock.

(c) Shortly before the contemplated transfer, *T* borrows $300 that it uses to redeem *B*'s *T* stock. *P* then assumes *X*'s $500 of liabilities, and issues $700 FMV of *P* voting common stock in exchange for the *T* assets.

(4) *T* merges into *S*, a newly formed, wholly owned subsidiary of *P*, solely for *P* voting stock, and *S* immediately liquidates.

11C Types D (Nondivisive) and F Reorganizations; Overlaps With § 304, § 351, and Liquidations

SUBJECT: The nondivisive Type D reorganization, as compared with § 304 "redemptions"—Liquidation-reincorporation—The Type F reorganization—§ 351 overlaps

ASSIGNMENT

B&E: ¶¶ 3.19, 3.20, 6.09, 9.09 (key), 11.08, 12.26 (key), 12.28 (key), 12.42, 12.63[2], 12.63[4], 12.64 (key), 14.22

Code: §§ 1(h)(11), 172(b)(1)(A), 304, 312(h)(2), 318, 351(c), 354(b), 357(c), 358(a), 368(a)(1)(D), 368(a)(1)(F), 368(a)(2)(A), 368(a)(2)(H), 368(b), 368(c), 381(a), 381(b), 1361(b)(2)(A)

Regs: §§ 1.301-1(1), 1.312-11(a), 1.331-1(c), 1.354-1(a), 1.368-1(b), 1.381(b)-1(a)(2)

Cases: Berghash v. CIR, 361 F2d 257 (2d Cir. 1966); Davant v. CIR, 366 F2d 874 (5th Cir. 1966) [*Note:* Type F can no longer apply to an exchange involving two operating corporations as in this case]; Aetna Casualty & Surety Co. v. US, 568 F2d 811 (2d Cir. 1976); Bercy Indus., Inc. v. CIR, 640 F2d 1058 (9th Cir. 1981); Telephone Answering Serv. Co., 63 TC 423 (1974), aff'd, 547 F2d 423 (4th Cir. 1976); Warsaw Photo Assocs., 84 TC 21 (1985)

Other materials: Rev. Rul. 61-156, 1961-2 CB 62; Rev. Rul. 70-240, 1970-1 CB 81; Rev. Rul. 75-161, 1975-1 CB 114; Rev. Rul. 79-289, 1979-2 CB 145; Rev. Rul. 84-71, 1984-1 CB 106; Rev. Rul. 2002-85, 2002-52 IRB 986; Rev. Proc. 77-37, 1977-2 CB 568; Rev. Proc. 86-42, 1986-2 CB 722

PROBLEMS

Assumptions: X and Y, though in different businesses, have the following identical characteristics: (1) $100 cash; (2) operating assets with a basis of $100 and FMV of $300; (3) no liabilities; (4) E&P of $100; and (5) single class of stock outstanding of 100 shares worth $4 per share. Assume that all persons are unrelated and all transactions are at arm's length and for FMV unless otherwise indicated. Where necessary, assume the existence of a plan of reorganization, a business purpose for the transaction, and continuity of business enterprise.

    In each problem below, determine any tax consequences to A, B, X, and Y.

(1)   A owns 45 shares of Y with an adjusted basis of $90. B owns 55 shares of Y with an adjusted basis of $110. A owns all the stock of X with an adjusted basis of $200. A sells his X stock to Y for cash and Y notes totaling $400.

    (a)   What if A and B are father and son?

    (b)   What if X sells its operating assets to Y for cash and Y notes totaling $300, after which time X dissolves?

    (c)   Alternatively to (b), what if X transfers all its operating assets to Y plus $60 cash in exchange for $360 FMV of nonvoting preferred stock of Y and no cash or notes, after which time X dissolves?

    (d)   Alternatively to (b), what if A and B are father and son?

    (e)   Alternatively to (b), what if A and B each own 50 shares of Y?

    (f)   What if Y sells its operating assets to X for $300 value ($120 cash and X notes and $180 FMV of X stock) and Y distributes the X stock to A and Y's cash and X notes totaling $220 to B in liquidation?

(2) A and B each own 50 shares in X and 50 shares in Y and each has an adjusted basis of $100 for the shares in X and Y, respectively. While X has $100 E&P, as in the basic assumption, Y now has none. X liquidates and A and B sell to Y the operating assets they receive from X for $300 in cash and notes. Y then elects S status.

Alternatives:

(a) X holds $300 cash, the value of X's operating assets is $100 (with a $50 basis), and X sells the assets to Y for $100 cash and then liquidates.

(b) A and B sell their X stock to Y for an aggregate $400 cash and notes (but now their X stock basis is $250 each) and, as part of the plan, X liquidates into Y. Y has $100 of E&P, but also has NOLs in years both before and after the sale, but X was profitable. Alternative: Y is an S corporation (without NOLs or E&P).

(c) Y is a newly organized corporation chartered in another state and has NOLs in the first tax year after the exchange.

(d) X's operating assets are subject to debts of $200 and X merges into Y for $200 FMV of Y stock.

(3) A and B each own 50 shares of X. X owns all 100 shares of Y. X is purely a holding company and merges down into Y, with A and B swapping their X stock for 50 shares each of Y stock.

Alternative: Only X exists and it causes Y to be incorporated. X then transfers all its assets subject to its debts to Y in exchange for all of the Y stock to be issued, after which time X liquidates. X has NOLs and owes debts of $200.

Triangular Reorganizations

SUBJECT: Types A, B, and C reorganizations involving more than one corporation on the acquirer side—Zero basis problems-Remote continuity of interest

ASSIGNMENT

B&E: ¶¶ 3.12; 9.01, 12.21[3], 12.22[3], 12.24[3][b], 12.24[4], 12.25 (key), 12.40[2], 12.43, 12.44[1], 12.63[6] (key), 12.65, 14.21[3], 14.23[2]

Code: §§ 304(a)(2), 317(b), 351, 357(a), 358(e), 362(a), 362(b), 368(a)(1)(A)–368(a)(1)(C), 368(a)(2)(B)–368(a)(2)(E), 368(b), 368(c), 381(a), 1032

Regs: §§ 1.358-4(a), 1.358-6, 1.362-1, 1.368-1(c), 1.368-1(d), 1.368-2(b), 1.368-2(c), 1.368-2(d), 1.368-2(f), 1.368-2(j), 1.368-2(k), 1.381(a)-1(b)(2), 1.1001-3(e)(4)(i), 1.1032-2, 1.1032-3

Cases: Groman v. CIR, 302 US 82 (1937); CIR v. Bashford, 302 US 454 (1938) [*Note:* These cases arose when there could be boot in a Type B reorganization.]

Other materials: Rev. Rul. 67-326, 1967-2 CB 143; Rev. Rul. 67-448, 1967-2 CB 144; Rev. Rul. 2001-24, 2001-22 IRB 1290; Rev. Rul. 2001-25, 2001-22 IRB 1291; Rev. Rul. 2001-26, 2001-23 IRB 1297; Rev. Rul. 2001-46, 2001-42 IRB 321; Rev. Rul. 2002-85, 2002-52 IRB 986

PROBLEMS

Assumptions: *T* has 100 shares of voting common stock outstanding, all owned by *A* (basis $700). *T* owns assets worth $1,200 with an adjusted basis of $900. *T* owes $200 and has E&P of $300. *P* is a publicly held corporation whose stock is traded on the NYSE. *S* is a wholly owned subsidiary of *P*. *P*'s basis in the *S* stock is $100 (except when facts state that *S* is newly incorporated). Assume that each *T* share is worth $10 and that property exchanged therefor is worth $10. Unless otherwise indicated, (1) each transaction has a proper business purpose, (2) there is a continuity of *T*'s "business enterprise," and (3) all steps of the transaction are pursuant to a "plan of reorganization."

In the problems below, what are the tax consequences to *A*, *T*, *S*, and *P*?

(1)   *T* transfers all its assets to *P* solely for $1,000 FMV of *P* voting stock and *P*'s assumption of *T*'s liabilities, after which time *T* liquidates. *P* immediately transfers the *T* assets to *S* (subject to the *T* liabilities) for additional *S* stock.

Alternative: Under the acquisition agreement between *T* and *P*, *T* must directly convey half its assets to *S* and half to *S1* (a new, wholly owned subsidiary of *S*). *S* and *S1* will each assume the $200 liabilities, which will remain secured by all the assets.

(2)   Pursuant to the acquisition agreement between *T* and *S*, *T* transfers all its assets to *S* (which assumes *T*'s liabilities) and *S* pays to *T* $1,000 FMV of *P* voting stock (which stock *P* had contributed to *S* to be used for this purpose).

Alternatives:

   (a)   *S* pays for the *T* assets with *P* stock *S* had bought in the market for $500 cash; alternatively, for $1,500 cash.

   (b)   *P* transfers $1,000 FMV of its voting stock directly to *T* pursuant to the acquisition agreement entered into by all three corporations.

(3)   *P* acquires directly from *A* all of *A*'s *T* stock solely in exchange for the transfer by *P* of $1,000 FMV of *P* voting stock. Immediately thereafter, *P* drops the *T* stock into *S* for no more stock.

Alternatives:

   (a)   Under a contract with *A*, *S* acquires the *T* stock directly from *A* and transfers *P* stock directly to *A*, which stock *P* previously had contributed to *S* for this purpose.

(b)   Continuing with (3)(a) above, S transfers the acquired T stock to S's newly created subsidiary, $S1$, in exchange for all of $S1$'s stock.

(c) $S1$ (S's wholly owned subsidiary) acquires all the T stock directly from A solely for P voting stock transferred to A by P.

(d) P transfers to A its voting stock worth $800, S transfers to A its voting stock worth $200, and A transfers all the T stock to S.

(4) P transfers its voting stock worth $1,000 to S (here, newly formed with no other capital) solely for stock of S. Immediately thereafter, S (whose only asset is the P stock) merges into T. Under the plan of merger and by operation of state law, the S stock owned by P is exchanged for one share of T stock; the T stock held by its shareholder A is exchanged for the P stock received by T on the merger of S into T. (As a result of these exchanges, P owns 100 percent of T.) What if, instead, there was no contribution by P of its stock to S but P simply transferred P stock directly to A.

Alternatives:

(a) A owns 85 percent and B owns 15 percent of the T stock. B dissents and P transfers $150 cash and $850 FMV of P voting stock to S, which cash and stock T exchanges with B and A, respectively. What if P promptly merges T upstream?

(b) P capitalized S with $1,000 cash, which T exchanged with A for A's T stock.

(c)   Could this transaction be effected as a § 368(a)(2)(E) merger if P already owned 21 percent of T? Suppose S redeems one percent of its stock held by P?

(d) P acquires half of the T stock for its voting stock and acquires the rest of the T stock by a reverse merger (again using P voting stock).

(5)   In a transaction that qualifies as a statutory merger under state law, S acquires all the assets of T (and assumes its liabilities) solely in exchange for $1,000 FMV of P nonvoting preferred stock (which previously had been contributed by P to S for this purpose). The merger plan provides that A's T stock will be canceled and the P stock will be issued to A and that S's shares remain outstanding in P's hands. What if, instead, there was no contribution by P of its stock to S?

Alternatives:

(a) S issues $400 of its 20-year bonds (and exchanges only $600 of P stock) in the transaction.

(b) S exchanges $40 FMV of its nonvoting preferred stock and $960 FMV of P voting stock in the transaction.

Alternative: S exchanges $960 FMV of its voting stock and only $40 of P's voting stock in the transaction.

(c) P transfers all of the S stock to newly organized S-2 shortly after the transaction in problem (5).

(d) T has two businesses of equal size; after acquiring T, S sells one of those businesses and reinvests the proceeds in the other business. Any difference if S uses some of the proceeds to pay off T's creditors? To pay a $500 "special dividend" to P?

Creeping Acquisitions [Advanced]

SUBJECT: The *Bausch & Lomb* doctrine and related problems—How the acquiror's prior ownership of some of the target stock can affect the tax consequences of a later stock or asset acquisition—Minority freezeout—Taxpayer invocation of the STD—Section 338 and Type F reorganization retrospective—The Service's abandonment of *Bausch & Lomb* by regulation (after forty years of taxpayer torture)

ASSIGNMENT

B&E: ¶¶ 10.05[4], 10.22, 10.24, 10.41–10.44, 12.22[4], 12.42[2], 12.61[3], 12.63[2] (key), 12.63[4], 12.63[5] (key)

Code: §§ 331, 332, 334, 336–338, 361, 362, 368(a)(1)(A), 368(a)(1)(C), 368(a)(2)(B), 368(a)(2)(E), 368(a)(2)(G), 1361(b)(2)(A), 1362(d)(2), 1362(f), 1371(a), 1374(d)(8)

Regs: §§ 1.332-2(d), 1.332-2(e), 1.332-5, 1.338-3(d), 1.338(h)(10)-1T (2003), 1.368-1(b), 1.368-2(a), 1.368-2(d)(4) (2000) (key)

Cases: Bausch & Lomb Optical Co. v. CIR, 267 F2d 75 (2d Cir. 1959); King Enters., Inc. v. US, 418 F2d 511 (Ct. Cl. 1969); American Potash & Chem. Corp. v. US, 399 F2d 194 (Ct. Cl. 1968); May B. Kass v. CIR, 60 TC 218 (1973); Yoc Heating Corp. v. CIR, 61 TC 168 (1973); J.E. Seagram Corp., 104 TC 75 (1995)

Other materials: Rev. Rul. 57-278, 1957-1 CB 124; Rev. Rul. 58-93, 1958-1 CB 188; Rev. Rul. 72-327, 1972-2 CB 19; Rev. Rul. 84-71, 1984-1 CB 106; Rev. Rul. 90-95, 1990-2 CB 67; Rev. Rul. 2001-26, 2001-23 IRB 1297; Rev. Rul. 2001-46, 2001-42 IRB 321; Rev. Rul. 2003-51, 2003-21 IRB 938

PROBLEMS

Assumptions: T is an operating company with assets worth $1,000 (basis $700) and no liabilities. T has $300 E&P. A owns some or all of the outstanding common stock of T, its only class, as stated in the various problems below. P is a publicly held operating company. Ignore the effect of tax on any gain recognized by T and assume T stock is worth $10 per share. Assume the existence of a good business purpose for the transactions, continuity of T's business enterprise, and a plan of reorganization where necessary (though the time boundaries of the plan may be at issue).

In each of the following transactions, what are the tax consequences to each of the parties?

The Big First Step, but Not "Control"

(1) P owns 70 percent of T (acquired 10 years ago for $200) and A owns 30 percent of T (basis $100).

Alternatives:

(a) P organizes a new subsidiary, S, and S merges into T, with T shareholders receiving P stock.

(b) T transfers all of its assets to P solely in exchange for voting stock of P; shortly thereafter, and as part of the plan, T liquidates, distributing 70 percent of its assets to P and 30 percent to A (which assets consist solely of P stock).

(c) T merges into P pursuant to state law and A receives $300 FMV of P nonvoting stock for the T shares. All outstanding T shares are canceled.

Alternative: P purchases its 70 percent interest for cash just before the merger.

(d) P acquires all of A's T stock solely for P voting stock worth $300.

(e)   *P* organizes a new subsidiary, *S*, and transfers its voting stock worth $1,000 to *S* in exchange for all of *S*'s stock. *T* then transfers all of its assets to *S* solely for the *P* stock, after which time *T* liquidates.

Alternative: *P* purchases the 70 percent for cash just before the merger.

The First Little Step

(2)   *P* owns 20 percent of the *T* stock (acquired 10 years ago for $100) and *A* owns 80 percent (basis $200). *T* transfers all its assets to *P* solely for $1,000 FMV of *P* voting stock, after which time *T* liquidates.

(3)   *B* owns 20 percent of *T* stock (basis $10), and *A* owns the rest. *B* contributes the 20 percent stock interest to newly formed *S* for pure preferred *S* stock, while *P* contributes $800 cash to *S* for all of *S*'s common stock. *T* then merges into *S*, with *A* receiving $800 cash and all *T* stock being canceled.

The First Step Obtains "Control"

(4)   *P* owns 80 percent of *T*'s outstanding stock, which *P* acquired 10 years ago (basis $200), and *A* owns 20 percent (basis $100). *T* transfers all its assets to *P* solely for $1,000 FMV of *P* voting stock, after which *T* liquidates.

(5)   *P* owns 80 percent of *T*'s outstanding stock, which *P* acquired 10 years ago (basis $200), and *A* owns 20 percent (basis $100). *T* merges into *P*, and *P* transfers $200 FMV of *P* stock to *A*. All outstanding *T* stock is canceled.

Alternatives:

(a)   *P* recently purchased the 80 percent for cash as part of the transaction.

(b)   Same as (a) above, but *T* merges into *S* a newly created, wholly owned subsidiary of *P*.

(c)   Same as (a) above, but *P* is a closely held S corporation and *T* is a C corporation.

Step Transaction Doctrine Variations (Multi-Step Stock and/or Asset Acquisitions)

(6)   In the following alternative transactions, *P* did not own any of *T*'s stock prior to the events in question. *A* owned all the *T* stock with a basis of $300.

(a)   *P* purchases 50 percent of *A*'s *T* stock for cash. Shortly thereafter, *T* transfers all its assets to *P* for $1,000 FMV of *P* voting stock, after which time *T* liquidates.

Alternative: After the stock purchase, *T* merges into *P* under state law, *A* receives $500 FMV of *P* stock, and the *T* stock is canceled.

(b)   *P* purchases all of *A*'s *T* stock for $500 cash and $500 FMV of *P* voting stock. Shortly thereafter, *T* merges into *P* pursuant to state law.

(c)   *P* acquires 50 percent of *A*'s *T* stock for $500 FMV of *P* voting stock. Fourteen months later, *P* decides to obtain control of *T* and acquires the balance of *A*'s *T* stock for $500 of *P* voting stock. As part of the same transaction (at least including the second stock purchase), *P* then liquidates *T* and operates its business as a division.

(d)   *T* is owned 15 percent by *B* and 85 percent by *A*; *P* buys *B*'s stock for cash and also acquires *A*'s *T* stock for *P* voting stock; *P* promptly merges *T* into its newly organized subsidiary, *S* (or vice versa). *Alternative*: *P* merges *T* up into *P* after acquiring all the *T* stock.

Note: You have just completed the Bermuda Triangle of the tax law. If your enthusiasm for same is still intact, we are ready to move on to the last lap, Corporate Divisions.

Corporate Divisions

SUBJECT: Converting the outstanding capital of one corporation into the capital of two (or more) corporations, in the hands of the original shareholders (but not necessarily pro rata), without gain recognition on either the corporate transfer(s) or the shareholder receipt of new stock—Unwanted assets in acquisition situations and bust up acquisitions—The divisive Type D reorganization [It is crucial to note that while a division may involve a D reorganization as a first step, it need not.]

ASSIGNMENT

B&E: Chapter 11 (key); ¶¶ 6.09[4], 9.07[3], 12.24[2], 12.26 (key), 12.62 (key for Q8), 14.21[3]

Code: §§ 302(b), 306(c)(1)(B), 311, 312(h), 336(c), 337(d), 346(b), 354(b), 355, 356(a)–356(c), 357(c), 358(a), 358(b), 361, 362(b), 368(a)(1)(C), 368(a)(1)(D), 368(a)(2)(A), 368(c), 381(a), 1032, 1361(b)(2)(A), 1362(b)(2), 1371(a), 1374(e)

Regs: §§ 1.312-10, 1.312-11(a), 1.355 (vital), 1.355-6 (re § 355(d)), 1.355-7T (re § 355(e) (key)), 1.358-2(a)(2), 1.358-2(a)(3), 1.368-1(b), 1.368-2T(b)(1) (2003)

Cases: Gregory v. Helvering, 293 US 465 (1935); South Tulsa Pathology Lab, Inc., 118 TC 84 (2002); Rafferty v. CIR, 452 F2d 767 (1st Cir. 1971); CIR v. Coady, 289 F2d 490 (6th Cir. 1961); Estate of Lockwood v. CIR, 350 F2d 712 (8th Cir. 1965); Douglas McLaulin, 115 TC 255 (2000), aff'd, 276 F3d 1269 (11th Cir. 2001); Helvering v. Elkhorn Coal Co., 95 F2d 732 (4th Cir. 1937); CIR v. Morris Trust, 367 F2d 794 (4th Cir. 1966)

Other materials: Rev. Proc. 96-30, 1996-1 CB 696 (ruling guidelines), modified by Rev. Proc. 2003-48, 2003-29 IRB 86; Rev. Rul. 70-434, 1970-2 CB 83; Rev. Rul. 70-

225, 1970-1 CB 80; Rev. Rul. 79-184, 1979-1 CB 143; Rev. Rul. 93-62, 1993-2 CB 118; Rev. Rul. 98-27, 1998-1 CB 1159; Rev. Rul. 98-44, 1998-2 CB 315; Rev. Rul. 2000-5, 2000-5 IRB 436; Rev. Rul. 2003-52, 2003-22 IRB 960; Rev. Rul. 2003-55, 2003-22 IRB 961; Rev. Rul. 2003-74, 2003-29 IRB 77; Rev. Rul. 2003-75, 2003-29 IRB 79; Rev. Rul. 2003-79, 2003-29 IRB 80

PROBLEMS

Assumptions: A and B each has owned 50 percent of the stock of X for many years. A's stock basis is $800 (FMV $1,000) and B's stock basis is $1,200 (FMV $1,000). X is engaged in two lines of business (and has been so engaged for the last five years, unless the facts specify otherwise): the manufacture and sale of electronic equipment (Electro division) and the manufacture and sale of air conditioners (Airco division). The assets of each division have an FMV of $1,000 and an adjusted basis of $500, no liabilities exist, and X has E&P of $1,000. Assume that 100 percent of the stock of a corporation is worth the net value of its assets, and ignore calculation of tax owed by X. Except where otherwise indicated, assume that the transactions are motivated by good corporate business purposes and that no shareholder plans to dispose of any stock received.

What are the tax consequences to the parties in each of the following transactions?

General Patterns

(1)   Split-up: X transfers all of the Electro assets to new Y in exchange for all of Y's stock and transfers all of the Airco assets to new Z in exchange for all of Z's stock. Immediately thereafter, X liquidates and distributes the Y stock and the Z stock ratably to A and B.

(a)   What if the business purpose was to allow Y to make an S election without fear that the substantial rental property dropped into Z (new facts) would trigger §§ 1362(d)(3) and 1375?

Alternative: What if the business purpose was to protect Airco assets from Electro creditors?

(b)   *Non–pro rata split-up:* What if *X* distributed the *Y* stock to *A* and the *Z* stock to *B*? What if *Y* sold its Electro business assets shortly after the distribution?

(c)   What if the value of the Electro business was $1,800, and the value of the Airco business was $200 (and *X* had NOL carryovers of $100)?

(2)   *Split-off:* *X* transfers the Electro assets to new *Y* in exchange for all of *Y*'s stock. Immediately thereafter, *X* distributes the *Y* stock to *A* in exchange for all of *A*'s *X* stock.

Alternative: What if Electro assets had been in *Y* for many years?

(a)   Would the result change if *A* had sold his stock to *C* for cash just after the split-off of *Y* to *A*? Just prior to the split-off of *Y* to *C*?

Alternative: What if the sale to *C* occurred two years prior to the division?

(b)   Spin-off: If *X* distributes the *Y* stock equally to *A* and *B*, what might the good corporate business purpose be?

Details

(3)   Vary the basic assumptions by assuming Electro and Airco were two separate corporations, each owned 50 percent by *A* and 50 percent by *B*. *A* and *B* transfer their stock in Electro and Airco to *X*, which shortly thereafter distributes the Electro stock to *A* and the Airco stock to *B*.

(4)   What would be the effect on question (2) above (without the alternative) if the basic assumptions were varied in the following alternative ways:

(a)   *X* was formed three years ago by a merger of Electro and Airco, which had been separate corporations.

(b)   *X* acquired the Airco assets three years ago in the following alternative ways:

(i)   For cash from a tax-exempt seller.

(ii)   For cash from a seller whose adjusted tax basis equaled the purchase price.

(iii) In a tax-free reorganization, but X paid $100 in cash boot as well.

(iv)   By liquidating Airco under §§ 332 and 337 immediately after having bought 100 percent of its stock for cash.

(5)   Assume that X has only the Electro business (FMV $1,000) and a long-held 70 percent stock interest in Airco, which owns the Airco business described in the basic assumptions. X transfers the Airco stock to Y in exchange for all of Y's stock and then distributes the Y stock equally to A and B.

Alternative: Suppose X first acquired an additional 10 percent of the Airco minority stock interest for cash? For its voting stock? By contributing property to Airco in exchange for Airco stock?

(6)   "Vertical" and "horizontal" or "functional" divisions: X has only the Electro business (asset value $2,000 and adjusted basis $1,000). A and B disagree and want to divide the assets between them. Pursuant to this plan, the following alternative events occur:

(a)   The assets of X are split "down the middle," and X transfers one half of the Electro assets to Y in exchange for all of Y's stock, which X then distributes to A in exchange for A's X stock. Would it matter if Y's half of the assets consisted of a separate plant and sales office in a different state that X had bought three years previously to expand its existing Electro business?

(b)   Because X has two Electro plants, one large and one small, when the small plant is transferred to Y, all of X's cash, receivables, and investment assets must also be transferred to Y to equalize the values of X and Y.

(c)   *X* spins off (pro rata to *A* and *B*) its sales department (worth $500).

(7)   *X* owns a 20-story building, wholly occupied (10 floors each) by the Electro and Airco divisions, and alternatively:

     (a)   The building alone is transferred to *Y* in exchange for all of *Y*'s stock, which is then distributed ratably to *A* and *B*. *Y* leases the building back to *X* on a triple net lease. Also, what if *X* has always been an S corporation? Can *Y* immediately elect S?

     (b)   The building (worth $1,000) and the Airco assets (worth $500) are transferred to *Y* in exchange for *Y*'s stock, which is then distributed ratably to *A* and *B*. *Y* leases part of the building (for the Electro business) back to *X* on a triple net lease.

Divisions and Acquisitions

(8)   "Unwanted assets." *P* (a publicly held corporation that is many times larger than *X*) desires to acquire the Airco business but not the Electro business; the following alternative transactions occur:

     (a)   *X* transfers the Electro assets to *Y* in exchange for all of *Y*'s stock and distributes the *Y* stock equally to *A* and *B*. Shortly thereafter, *P* acquires all of the *X* stock from *A* and *B* for $1,000 cash.

     Alternatives:

          (i)   Shortly after the spin-off, *P* acquires all of the Airco assets from *X* for $1,000 FMV of its voting stock, and *X* liquidates.

          (ii)   *X* merges into *P* shortly after spinning off the Electro business, with *A* and *B* receiving a small minority share of *P* common stock.

(iii)   *X* drops the Airco business into *Y* and spins it off pro rata. Shortly thereafter, *Y* merges into *P*, with *A* and *B* receiving a small minority share of *P* stock.

(iv)   Would the results in (8)(a)(iii) above differ if *Y* (holding Airco assets) was an old and cold subsidiary?

(v)   Continue with (8)(a)(iii) and (8)(a)(iv) above, but assume that *P* merges into *Y*, with *Y* surviving and *P* shareholders receiving the large majority share of *Y* stock.

(vi)   What results if *P* is the "smaller" of the two merging corporations?

(vii)   What results if the mergers occur more than two years after the spin-off? More than six months?

(b)   *P* buys all of the *X* stock for $2,000 cash and causes *X* to drop the unwanted Electro assets into new *Y* and to spin-off the *Y* stock to *P*. Thereafter, *P* will sell the *Y* stock for $1,000 (presumably, at no gain, if the *X* stock basis is split between the *X* and *Y* stock).

Recapitalizations (Part Two) [Very Advanced]

SUBJECT: Reorganizations that change the capital structure of a single corporation by its exchanges of new stock for outstanding stock (see Lesson 7C), debt for debt, stock for debt, debt for stock, and combinations

Note: Recapitalizations also routinely involve § 305, § 306, COD, and OID.

ASSIGNMENT

B&E: ¶¶ 4.03[5], 4.25, 4.40–4.42, 4.44, 4.60–4.62, 8.41, 8.62, 8.63, 8.65, 12.21[6], 12.26[2], 12.27 (key), 12.30[5], 12.41, 12.44, 12.45

Code: §§ 1(h)(11), 61(a)(12), 108(a), 108(b), 108(d)(3), 108(e), 163(e), 171, 249, 301, 302, 305, 306(b)(3), 306(c)(1)(B), 306(c)(1)(C), 312(d), 354, 356, 358(a), 358(b)(1), 368(a)(1)(E), 382(g)(3)(A), 382(k)(6)(A), 453(f)(4), 453(f)(5), 453(f)(6), 453(k)(2)(A), 1001, 1012, 1031, 1032, 1036, 1272–1274, 1275(a)(4), 1276(c)(2)(B), 1278(a)(1)(D), 1278(a)(2)(A)

Regs: §§ 1.61-12(a), 1.61-12(c), 1.163-4(c), 1.301-1(1), 1.305-7(c), 1.306-1(b)(1), 1.306-3(d), 1.312-1(e), 1.354-1, 1.356-1, 1.356-3, 1.358-1, 1.358-2, 1.368-2(e), 1.1001-1(a), 1.1002-1(c), 1.1001-3, 1.1031(b)-1(a)(3), 1.1036-1, 1.354-1(e), 1.356-3(b)

Cases: Wm. H. Bateman, 40 TC 408 (1963); Neville Coke & Chem. Co. v. CIR, 148 F2d 599 (3d Cir.), cert. denied, 326 US 726 (1945); Bazley v. CIR, 331 US 737 (1947); National Alfalfa Dehydrating & Milling Co., 417 US 134 (1974); Gulf M&O R.R. v. US, 579 F2d 892 (5th Cir. 1978); Cottage Savings Ass'n v. CIR, 499 US 554, 111 S. Ct. 1503 (1991)

Other materials: Rev. Rul. 90-11, 1990-1 CB 10

PROBLEMS

Assumptions: The exchanges effected in these problems are pursuant to a "plan" of reorganization and have a good business purpose (although the transactions do not necessarily qualify as Type E reorganizations). In all cases, the stock and debt referred to are issued by X and are properly characterized as such. There is ample E&P, and the face amount of any debt is also its stated redemption price at maturity (SRPM). A is a cash method taxpayer and X uses the accrual method.

In each problem (except as otherwise indicated) determine the tax consequences of the described exchanges to the affected debt holders and shareholders and to X.

Note: For problems on the type of recapitalizations involving new stock for old stock, see Lesson 7C.

New Stock for Old Debt (Stock-For-Debt Swaps)

(1) X, which is in financial difficulty but not insolvent, is able to improve its balance sheet and its economic health by repurchasing $10 million face amount (and adjusted issue price) of its outstanding publicly traded bonds (having no unpaid accrued stated periodic interest or OID) for a new issue of pure preferred stock (nonvoting, nonparticipating, nonconvertible; see § 382(k)(6)(A)) worth $8 million. The stock has liquidation rights and is callable by X, at its issue price. What would result to X and the bond holders?

Alternatives:

(a) X effected the discharge in a title 11 case. Alternative: X issued only $100,000 in stock value in cancellation of the bonds.

(b)   What would result to X and the bondholders (assume an aggregate $10 million basis in the bonds) if X also issued warrants worth $500,000 granting rights to buy its common stock in the transaction in (1) above. What if old warrants held by the bondholders are swapped for new warrants?

(c)   What would result to the debtholders if the discharged debt consisted of five-year notes. What if X is insolvent? [*Hint*: Alabama Asphaltic.]

(d)   What would result to X and the bondholders if the exchange was pursuant to a conversion privilege contained in the bonds?

(e)   Would the COD result to X change if the $10 million (face amount, but query the adjusted issue price) in bonds had been issued 5 years ago in exchange for preferred stock then worth $10 million that X had issued 10 years before that for $5 million?

(2) A exchanges the bond of solvent X that A acquired at original issue (with a face amount, adjusted basis, and adjusted issue price of $1,000, $100 accrued stated periodic interest, FMV of $1,200) for preferred stock of X worth $1,200. What if the bond's basis and adjusted issue price were $800?

Alternatives:

(a)   What if the stock and bond FMV are $500 and X is in a title II case?

(b)   What if A's basis in the bond is $800 as the result of a purchase in the market, $100 market discount has accrued, and there is no unpaid accrued interest?

(c)   What if A had received the bond from X in a § 453 installment sale?

New Debt for Old Stock (Debt-For-Stock Swaps)

(3) X redeems all its outstanding publicly traded nonconvertible, nonparticipating preferred stock (representing 65 percent of the equity value of X) by issuing 20-year bonds. One of the shareholders, A, exchanges preferred stock of X (not § 306 stock) worth $1,000 (basis $900, derived by purchase from X upon original issue) for a $1,000 (face and FMV) bond in this transaction. Would it make a difference if neither the stock nor the bond were publicly traded and the bond bore "adequate stated interest"?

Alternatives:

(a)   What if the stock and bond are worth $800?

(b)   What if the bond bore no interest and had a face amount of $5,000 and FMV of $1,000?

New Debt and Stock for Old Stock (Debt-For-Stock Swap Variations)

(4)   *A*, the only shareholder of *X*, aiming for do-it-yourself integration, exchanges some of *X*'s voting common stock (basis $100, FMV $500), for a new class of voting common stock worth $200 and long-term bonds with a face amount, issue price, and value of $300. What if, instead, *A* is not the sole shareholder and the exchanges are made pro rata by all *X* shareholders?

Alternatives:

(a)   What if *A* is a 5 percent common shareholder whose percentage of the vote drops to 2 percent after the exchange?

(b)   What if *A*'s basis in the *X* stock transferred was $300 instead of $100?

(c)   What if *X* has no E&P?

New Debt for Old Debt (Debt Swaps)

(5)   *A* exchanges a publicly traded (meaning "traded on an established securities market") bond of *X* issued after July 18, 1984, due in 10 years, with an FMV and face amount of $1,000 (its original and adjusted issue prices) and an adjusted basis of $800, in exchange for a new, identical publicly traded bond issued to *A* by *X*, worth its face amount of $1,000, due 20 years after the issuance of the original bond. The extension of the term does not significantly increase the risk of holding the bond. Assume that both bonds are "securities."

Alternatives:

(a)   The adjusted issue price of the old bond and *A*'s adjusted basis (from purchase at original issue) are $800, and the "qualified periodic interest" payable on the new bond is increased to produce the same overall yield to maturity as on the old bond.

(b)   Due to the shaky condition of *X*, the value of the old bond dropped to $600 and *A* exchanged the old bond for a new bond of *X* with face amount of $750 and FMV of $600. *X* has substantial NOLs. Assume that *A*'s adjusted basis in the old bond is $1,000.

Alternatives:

(i)   What if neither bond is publicly traded and the new bond pays "adequate stated interest"?

(ii)   What if *X* has no NOLs but effects the debt swap while in title 11?

(c)   The old bonds have 16 percent "qualified periodic interest" but are trading at $700 because the market doubts *X*'s ability to pay the interest. As part of an overall restructuring, the old bonds are exchanged for new bonds with a $1,100 face amount, paying 10 percent "qualified periodic interest." Because the market believes this debt can be serviced. the new bond also trades at $700. *A*'s adjusted basis in the old bond is $600.

(d)   Because of an improvement in *X*'s credit worthiness and a drop in interest rates, the old bond is worth $1,100 and *A* exchanges it for a new bond issued by *X* also worth $1,100, face amount of $1,200 and having lower "qualified periodic interest." Assume that the old bond's adjusted issue price and *A*'s adjusted basis in it are $800.

Corporate Tax Attributes: Survival and Transfer [Advanced]

SUBJECT: Mainly limits on the NOL and capital loss carryover outside the bankruptcy context and outside consolidated returns

ASSIGNMENT

B&E: Chapter 14 (most important, especially ¶¶ 14.41, 14.43 and 14.44); ¶¶ 2.11, 4.22[4], 6.06[3], 6.06[4], 10.20–10.24, 10.41, 10.42, 11.12[5], 12.61[1]

Code: Primary: §§ 269, 381(a)–381(c) (scan), 382 (key), 384; Ancillary: §§ 172(a), 172(b)(1)(A), 172(b)(1)(E), 172(b)(2), 172(c), 172(h), 332(a), 334(b), 338 (scan), 383, 446(b), 1212(a)(1), 1363(b)(2), 1366(a)(1)(B), 1366(d)(1), 1366(d)(2), 1371(b), 1374(b)(2), 1504(a)(4)

Regs: §§ 1.269, 1.382-2, 1.382-2T, 1.383-1 [*Note:* The temporary regulations under § 382 are tough going, but try to wade through them because they are vital to this lesson. Other relevant § 382 regulations are noted in B&E Chapter 14 discussion of § 382.]

Cases: Briarcliff Candy Corp., 54 TCM 667 (1987); Libson Shops, Inc. v. Koehler, 353 US 382 (1957); CIR v. British Motor Car Distributors, Ltd., 278 F2d 392 (9th Cir. 1960); Textron, Inc. v. US, 561 F2d 1023 (1st Cir. 1977)

Other materials: Rev. Rul. 63-40, 1963-1 CB 46

PROBLEMS

Note: Assume throughout these problems that affiliated corporations do not file consolidated returns.

Overview of Loss Deduction Limitations

(1)   *A* has always owned all of the common stock of *L*, *L*'s only class of stock outstanding. *L* operates a retail store that has been losing money (although it broke even this year) and has a total of $1 million in NOL carryovers expiring in part during each of the next 10 to 15 years. Unrelated *P* operates a profitable manufacturing business (which earns $500,000 this year after the alternative transactions described below) and owns a substantial amount of highly appreciated assets. What effect does each of the following transactions have on *L*'s NOL carryover? (The key throughout these problems is what happens to *A* – *A* is the pea under the pod.)

   (a)   *A* contributes sufficient capital to *L* so that *L* can buy *P*'s profitable manufacturing business (all of *P*'s assets).

   (b)   *L* sells all its assets to *X* and uses the proceeds to buy the profitable manufacturing business from *P*.

   (c)   *A* has always owned all of the *P* stock. *A* causes *P* to merge into *L*.

   (d)   *L* acquires the stock of *P* from an unrelated party for cash and causes *P* to liquidate. *L* begins to operate *P*'s profitable manufacturing business.

   Alternatives:

   (i)   What if *P* acquires *L* stock for cash and makes a § 338 election?

   (ii)   What if *P* acquires *L* stock for cash and, with *A* Corporation, makes a § 338(h)(10) election?

98

(iii)   What if *P* acquires *L* stock for cash and liquidates *L*?

(iv)   What if *P* acquires *L* stock for cash and liquidates *L*, which is insolvent (meaning FMV of assets is exceeded by liabilities)?

(e)   *P* buys all of the stock of *L* for cash and makes a cash capital contribution to *L* so that *L* can revive its retail business, make money, and avoid income tax by using its NOL. Additionally (and alternatively), suppose *P* made these cash payments with borrowed money and incurred a NOL in this year due to *P*'s high interest expense.

(f)   *L* merges into *B*'s wholly owned corporation, *P*, and *A* receives 49 percent of the outstanding common stock of *P* (its only class).

(g)   *A* sells all of the *L* stock to *B* and *B* causes *L* to make an S election.

Note: While §§ 269 and 384 may apply to the following questions, we will ignore them in order to focus on § 382.

The § 382 Limitation (B&E ¶ 14.44)

(2)   *L* has business assets worth $8 million and NOL carryovers of $1 million expiring in 14 years and of $2 million expiring in 15 years, and 100 percent of *L*'s stock is worth $10 million (why?). If *L* sells its business assets without recognizing gain or loss, *L* can invest its $8 million liquid assets in U.S. Treasury bonds earning 10 percent so that *L* can use its NOLs at the rate of $800,000 per year. The long-term tax-exempt rate is 8 percent. What will "the § 382 limitation" be if an ownership change occurs with respect to *L*'s stock?

Alternative: What if *L* has minimal assets and 100 percent of its stock is worth $1 million?

(3)   *T* is a publicly held operating corporation that has wholly owned operating subsidiaries *T-1*, *T-2*, and *T-3*. *T* and its subsidiaries have all sustained NOLs;

moreover, their assets have substantially declined in value below adjusted basis.

P is a publicly held operating corporation that has wholly owned operating subsidiaries *P-1*, *P-2*, and *P-3*. *P* and its subsidiaries are all profitable and all have substantially appreciated assets (unless otherwise stated).

In each of the following alternatives, assume that the application of the § 382 limitation has been triggered by an ownership change due to the described stock sale or merger (and thus an ownership change for *T* also will result in an ownership change for its subsidiaries, as will be studied in more detail in the next group of questions). State whether, and if so, how, the § 382 limitation will be applied to *T*'s (or *T*'s subsidiary's) NOLs.

(a)   *P* buys all of *T*'s stock, and *T* shortly thereafter sells its operating business for cash at a large loss and sells its portfolio stock at a gain.

Alternatives:

(i)   The sales occur three years later and yield a $500 net loss that had been inherent in the assets at the time of *P*'s purchase of the *T* stock.

(ii)   Continuing (3)(a)(i) above, *T*'s sales produce a net gain of $100 that had been inherent in the assets at the time of *P*'s purchase.

(b)   *T* sells its operating business for cash and invests the proceeds in its subsidiaries, *T-1*, *T-2*, and *T-3*. Subsequently, *P* acquires all the stock of *T*.

(c)   *T* sells all the stock of loss subsidiary *T-1* to *P* for cash (at a capital loss that *T* cannot use this year or carry back) a year-and-a-half after having incorporated *T-1* with built-in loss assets. *T-1* had substantial losses while *T* owned *T-1*. What additional loss limitation will apply to *T* in this case?

100

(d)   *T-1* merges into *P-1* on July 1 when *T-1* has NOLs that will expire in the third year after the current year. The § 382 limitation is $1,000 per year, the total NOLs carried over from *T-1* are $10,000, and only $500 of the NOLs was used by *P-1* in the last half of the calendar year of merger. On July 1 of the next year, *P-1* merges into *P* (not an ownership change). What NOLs can *P* use?

(4)   *T*, an S corporation, has an "ordinary loss from trade or business activities" this year. On the first day of next year, *B* acquires all of the *T* stock from *A*. Which taxpayer uses the loss and how?

The § 382 Trigger (B&E ¶ 14.43)

(5)   Continuing with the facts in (3) above, *T*'s public shareholder group (no one of whom owns 5 percent of *T*) is referred to as *A*, while *P*'s shareholder group (no one of whom owns 5 percent of *P*) is referred to as *B*. *A* and *B* (and *T* and *P*) are unrelated, unless otherwise stated. All corporations have only one class of stock (common) outstanding, unless otherwise stated. Is the § 382 limitation triggered by the following events?

(a)   *T* has a public offering of (what becomes) 60 percent of its stock to a new group of investors, *C*, none of whom owns 5 percent of *T*.

(i)   Suppose that one shareholder that otherwise would have been part of *T*'s *A* group instead owned 10 percent of *T* before the public offering (and dropped to 4 percent after).

(ii)   Suppose that one of the *C* group acquires 6 percent of *T* in the public offering.

(iii) Suppose that *P* is the person that acquires the *T* stock.

(iv)   Suppose that *C* only gets 20 percent of the *T* stock. What must *T* do?

(b)   *T* merges into *P*, after which *A* owns 40 percent of the surviving *P*.

        (i)   Alternatively, *A* owns 60 percent of the surviving *P*, but twelve months later *P* sells stock in an offering to *C* sufficient to give *C* 50 percent of the stock value and reduce the *A* group to 30 percent. In addition, suppose the value of the stock fluctuates daily.

        (ii)   What if in (5)(b)(i) above the *A* group had acquired one half of its stock two and one half years before the *T-P* merger?

        (iii)   *A* and *B* are wholly owned subsidiaries of *X*.

        (iv)   Alternatively, *T* merges into *P*'s newly organized subsidiary, *P-1*, for *P* stock (equal to 10 percent of *P*).

        (v)   Alternatively, though *A* owns 60 percent of the surviving *P*, *T* has stock options outstanding which, if exercised, would give the optionees 20 percent of the survivor and the *B* group 50 percent of the survivor. Separately, assume that the options later all lapsed unexercised.

        (vi)   Suppose that *A* and *B* were related individuals under § 318(a)(1). Would § 269 apply?

(c)   *A* and *B* contribute their *T* and *P* stock to new corporation N in exchange for N stock, after which *A* owns all of the common stock of N and *B* owns only pure preferred stock of N worth 60 percent of N's total capital. What if the preferred had a redemption price in excess of its issue price?

(d)   Assume that *T* is owned by two unrelated shareholders, *A* (60 percent) and *C* (40 percent), and *T* redeems all of *A*'s *T* stock for cash or notes.

Alternatives:

(i)   *T* distributes all the stock of one of its subsidiaries, *T-1*, to *A* in exchange for all of *A*'s *T* stock. Section 355 applies to the exchange.

(ii)   *T* incorporates its operating business in new subsidiary *T-4*, and then completely liquidates, distributing all of its subsidiaries, *T-1*, *T-2*, *T-3*, and *T-4*, ratably to *A* and *C* in an exchange to which § 355 applies.

(e)   *T* is owned 50-50 by *X* and *Y*. Neither *X* nor *Y* has a 5 percent shareholder other than its public group. Both *X* and *Y* have a common shareholder, *D*, who owns 6 percent of *T* by attribution. *D* purchases some more shares of *Y* in the market next year. Must *T* report that a testing date has occurred?

Insolvency Reorganizations (Type G) and Related Matters [Advanced]

SUBJECT: Corporations in title 11 bankruptcy ("or similar case") and their bankruptcy and tax "reorganization"—NOL preservation in such cases §§ 269 and 382 revisited—COD aspects of bankruptcy

ASSIGNMENT

B&E: ¶¶ 4.25 (key), 6.06, 6.10 (key), 12.21, 12.26[2], 12.27[3], 12.30 (key), 12.61, 14.44[6] (key), 14.44[7]

Code: Primary: §§ 108 (particularly §§ 108(a), 108(b), 108(d)(2), 108(d)(7), 108(e)(7), 108(e)(8), and 108(e)(10)), 368(a)(1)(G), 368(a)(3), 382(1)(5) (as effective in 1995), 382(1)(6), 1017; Ancillary: §§ 61(a)(12), 165(g), 166(a), 269, 312(1), 351(d)(2), 351(e)(2), 354, 355, 356, 361, 362, 368(a)(2)(C), 368(a)(2)(D), 368(a)(2)(E), 381(a), 381(b), 1060, 1366, 1367, 1399, 6658

Regs: §§ 1.108-2, 1.108-7T (2003), 1.269-3, 1.269-5, 1.269-7, 1.368-1(b), 1.368-1(d), 1.382-9, 1.1001-3, 1.1017-1T (2003), 1.1366-1(a)(2)(viii), 1.6012-2(a)(2) [*Note:* Other relevant regulations are cited in applicable paragraph sections of B&E.]

Cases: Helvering v. Alabama Asphaltic Limestone Co., 315 US 179 (1942); Centennial Savings Bank, 111 S. Ct. 1512 (1991); David Zarin v. CIR, 916 F2d 110 (3d Cir. 1990); Gitlitz v. CIR, 182 F3d 1143 (10th Cir. 1999), rev'd, 531 US 206 (2001)

Other Material: Rev. Rul. 59-222, 1959-2 CB 80; Senate Report on the Bankruptcy Tax Act of 1980, 1980-2 CB 620, 638-640

STUDY PROBLEMS

PROBLEMS

Assumptions: T is the petitioning debtor in a "title 11 case" under Chapter 11 (Reorganizations) of the Bankruptcy Code (except where Chapter 7 is specifically designated), and the various transactions described below are effected pursuant to a court-approved plan in that proceeding (which where necessary also constitutes a plan of tax reorganization). Immediately prior to the transactions described below, T has the following tax characteristics:

1. Depreciable operating business assets (adjusted basis $400,000, FMV $600,000);

2. Nondepreciable business assets, being land (adjusted basis $200,000, FMV $400,000);

3. Long-term debenture bonds long outstanding in the face amount (and adjusted basis to cash method holders) of $1 million, with unpaid interest of $200,000 that accrued and was deducted by T during the two years before bankruptcy was filed earlier this year;

4. Trade debt of $500,000 that arose before bankruptcy in the ordinary course of business of the current holders and that has been accrued into the holders income and not written off by them as a bad debt;

5. NOL carryovers of $500,000 expiring in 10 to 15 years (even though in an effort to reduce debts, T has sold a substantial amount of appreciated assets immediately prior to filing for bankruptcy); and

6. E&P deficit of $300,000.

Assume that T's historic business activity continues during and after the bankruptcy so as to pass any continuity of business enterprise test. T shareholders receive nothing and their stock is canceled. Note that § 1141(d) of the Bankruptcy Code provides that the confirmation of a plan of bankruptcy reorganization by the bankruptcy court discharges the debtor's debts, except as otherwise provided in the plan or in the order confirming the plan. Conversely, if there is no plan of bankruptcy reorganization under Chapter 11 of Title 11, but rather the corporation is liquidated under Chapter 7, there is no formal discharge of a bankrupt corporation's debts. The corporation simply liquidates without paying all its debts.

(1)   What are the tax consequences to the respective parties when T transfers all of its assets (free of T's debts) to P in exchange for the following alternative consideration (all of which is distributed by T as described below) and T liquidates:

   (a) $900,000 cash, $600,000 of which is distributed to T's bondholders and $300,000 of which is distributed to its trade creditors. P is an unrelated corporation and T is in a Chapter 7 case.

   Alternative: T has always been an S corporation and has no NOLs or E&P deficit, although $500,000 of "nonseparately computed" (operating) losses have passed through to T's shareholders in recent years. Assume the shareholders exhausted their stock basis by deducting $200,000 of those losses and the rest of the losses are suspended under § 1366(d).

   (b) $900,000 face and FMV of P's long-term bonds, $600,000 of which is distributed to T's bondholders and $300,000 of which is distributed to T's trade creditors. P is an unrelated corporation and T is in a Chapter 7 case.

   (c) $900,000 FMV of P preferred stock, $600,000 of which is distributed to the bondholders (and the plan specifically states that all stock is allocated to payment of principal) and $300,000 of which is distributed to the trade creditors, in discharge of all of their claims against T. P was organized by the T creditors, who own all of its common stock and now own all of P's stock. The preferred stock is nonvoting, is callable by P after 10 years at its FMV at the date of issue, and has a liquidation preference in the same amount.

Alternatives:

(i) *T* has NOL carryovers of $900,000.

(ii) *P* assumes the bond debt and pays $300,000 FMV preferred stock to the trade creditors in discharge of all of their claims against *T*. Would the results change if *T* shareholders received 50 percent of the outstanding *P* common stock?

(iii) *T*'s historic business shut down during the bankruptcy and *P* used the *T* assets to start a new business.

(iv) *T* has always been an S corporation with same additional facts as in the alternative question (1)(a) above.

(d) $600,000 FMV of nonvoting preferred of *P* is distributed to *T*'s bondholders and $300,000 FMV of *P*'s long-term bonds is distributed to *T*'s trade creditors in discharge of all claims against *T*. *P* is an unrelated corporation. The preferred is not redeemable and has a liquidation preference equal to its FMV at the date of issue.

(2) What would be the effect on your answers in question (1)(c) above if, alternatively:

(a) *P* immediately retransfers the *T* assets to its newly created subsidiary, *S*?

(b) *T* transfers its assets directly to *P*'s controlled subsidiary *S* for the described consideration paid by *P*?

(c) The transaction is structured as a "reverse merger" of *P*'s controlled subsidiary *S* into *T* for the consideration described. Would the result change if *T* shareholders get some *P* warrants?

(d) *T* split itself up in a divisive Type G reorganization?

LESSON **18**

Introduction To Affiliated Corporations [Advanced]

SUBJECT: Introduction to § 482 transactions between related corporations — Introduction to consolidated returns

ASSIGNMENT

B&E: Chapter 13; ¶ 8.05[10]

Code: §§ 267(f), 482, 542(b), 1501–1504, 1561–1563

Regs: §§ 1.267(f)-2, 1.482-1, 1.482-2, 1.482-3, 1.482-4, 1.482-5, 1.482-6, 1.482-7, 1.1502-2, 1.1502-11–1.1502-13, 1.1502-15, 1.1502-19, 1.1502-20, 1.1502-21, 1.1502-31, 1.1502-32, 1.1502-33, 1.1502-34, 1.1502-35T (2003) (just try to get the single-loss idea out of the preamble, i.e., the affiliated group is entitled to only one economic loss), 1.1502-76, 1.1502-79

Cases: Woods Investment Co., 85 TC 274 (1985); Sunstrand Corp., 95 TC 226 (1991); Rite Aid Corp. v. US, 255 F3d 1357 (Fed. Cir. 2001)

Other materials: Rev. Rul. 78-83, 1978-1 CB 79

PROBLEMS

Section 482

Assumptions: P is a U.S. corporation with two domestic subsidiaries, X and Y. P and its subsidiaries do not file consolidated returns.

What are the tax consequences of the following alternative transactions?

(1)   Loan transactions:

     (a) P loaned $100 to X without interest.

     (b) X loaned $100 to Y without interest.

     (c) Y loaned $100 to X at 30 percent interest.

(2)   Service transactions:

     (a) P rendered planning services (not its normal business) to X in connection with a proposed venture being looked into by X, at a cost to P of $100. X did not pay P for these services; had the services been rendered to an independent party, however, P would have charged $250. The proposed venture was not entered into by X.

     (b)   Suppose that the services rendered by P in (2)(a) above were of the type customarily performed by P in its business;

     (c)   Suppose that P's president incurred $100 of travel expenses while visiting X and Y to review their operations in order to report to P's directors. A copy of this report was also sent to the subsidiaries.

(3)   Leasing transactions: P leased one of its machines to Y for $10 a year. The machine was worth $1,000 at the time of this transaction.

(4)   Intangibles transactions: *P* developed and patented an industrial process, which it made available to its two subsidiaries free of charge. *P* also granted licenses for the use of this process to unrelated parties at a $10-a-year minimum royalty plus 10 percent of gross receipts.

Consolidated Returns

In (5) and (6) below, which corporations (if any) are includable in the filing of a consolidated return?

(5)   *P* owns all the stock of *X*; *A* owns all the stock of *P* and *Y*;

(6)   *P* owns all of *X* and *Y* common stock, but *A* owns all of *X* and *Y* nonconvertible, nonvoting preferred stock, which has a redemption price and liquidation preference equal to its issue price.

In all following questions, assume that consolidated returns are properly filed by the described corporations as an affiliated group. Ignore federal income tax accrued in determining a corporation's E&P. Assume that taxable income and E&P are the same except where the facts indicate otherwise.

(7)   *P* (a holding company) has three wholly owned operating subsidiaries, *X*, *Y*, and *Z*. *P*'s basis for its stock in *X*, *Y*, and *Z* (one class only) is $10, $20, and $30, respectively. During the year, the following transactions occur (*P*, *X*, *Y*, and *Z* had no intercompany transactions):

	X	*Y*	*Z*
Net ordinary business income	$200	$60	$40
§ 1231 gains	100	---	20
§ 1231 losses	---	20	---
Capital gains	20	---	10
Capital losses	30	---	---
§ 170 contributions	50	---	---

What is the group's consolidated taxable income?

(8)   P has two wholly owned subsidiaries, X and Y. What are the results from these events:

    (a)   P pays $20 of annual rent to X, and X and Y pay $10 and $5 of interest, respectively, to P.

    (b)   P sells land having a basis of $40 to X for $60; X later resells the land to an unrelated party for $70.

        (i)   What if P elected § 453?

        (ii)   What if X elected § 453?

    (c)   Suppose the property sold to X in (8)(b) above was depreciable property (used by X in its operations and not sold), and X utilized straight-line depreciation thereon with a useful life of 10 years (no salvage).

    (d)   Suppose the property in (8)(b) had a tax basis to P of $80.

(9)   P creates X, a wholly owned subsidiary. P's initial basis for its stock in X (one class) is $100 (before any adjustments). Determine the tax consequences to P and X from the following alternative transactions:

    (a)   X earns $20 and makes no distributions. Next year, X earns $10 and distributes $30 in cash to P. If P's only shareholder is A, could P be a personal holding company?

    (b)   Same as (9)(a) except P and X filed separate returns for both years.

    (c)   Same as (9)(a) except X's distribution to P consisted of portfolio securities (basis $10, value $30).

(10)   P creates X and Y (each having only one class of stock), and P, X, and Y file a consolidated return for that year. P's initial stock basis for X is $50 and for Y is $100.

LESSON 18

Alternatives:

(a)   For Year 1, *P* earns $100, *X* earns $10, and *Y* has operating losses of $20. What are the results?

     (i)   What if, in (10)(a) above, *X* distributes $5 to *P*.

     (ii)   What if, in (10)(a) above, *X* distributes $15 to *P* (which *P* contributes to *Y*)?

(b)   Assume the same facts for Year 1 as (10)(a). In Year 2, *P* earns $100, *X* has a $30 capital loss and $10 of ordinary income, and *Y* has operating losses of $15. Assume the capital loss cannot be carried back. *Alternative*: *P* had $30 of capital gain in Year 1.

(c)   For Year 1, *P* earns $10, *X* breaks even, and *Y* has operating losses of $15 (no carryback is available). *P* sells *Y*'s stock for $110 on December 31 of Year 1.

(d)   For Year 1, *X* has $25 separate taxable income but has $30 E&P because of *X*'s use of a slower depreciation method required for E&P purposes by § 312(k). Assume the investment basis adjustment (IBA) for Year 1 results in a $130 basis in the *X* stock. On the first day of Year 2, *P* sells the *X* stock for $125. How much gain or loss will *P* recognize on the sale?

(e)   On January 1 of Year 1, *P* buys *Z* stock for $150. For Year 1, *Z* has E&P of $50. *Z* pays a $50 cash dividend on December 31 of Year 1, and on January 1 of Year 2, *P* sells the *Z* stock for $100. Alternatively, what if the stock sale price is $80?

(11)   *P* and its wholly owned subsidiary *X* (created by *P*) have the following results for Years 1 and 2: *P* earns $100 for Year 1 and $50 for Year 2, while *X* has operating losses of $80 in Year 1 and $70 in Year 2. *P*'s initial basis for its *X* stock was $100.

STUDY PROBLEMS

(a)   If P sells its X stock on January 1 of Year 3 for $75, what are the results?

Alternative: What if A owned 20 percent of X's stock?

(b)   If P liquidates X under § 332 on January 1 of Year 3, what are the results? What if X is insolvent when it liquidates?

(c)   If P merges downstream into X on January 1 of Year 3, what are the results? Suppose instead that P distributes the X stock under § 355? Any difference if P's sole shareholder was corporate parent A?